Astrological Cycles In Focus

How astrological cycles predict events in your life.

Astrological Cycles In Focus

How astrological cycles predict events in your life.

Sasha Fenton

Zambezi Publishing Ltd
www.zampub.com

First published in 2021 in the UK by Zambezi Publishing Ltd
Plymouth, Devon PL2 2YJ
Tel: +44 (0)1752 367 300   Fax: +44 (0)1752 350 453
email: info@zampub.com   www.zampub.com

Text copyright ©2022 Sasha Fenton
Sasha Fenton has asserted the moral right to be identified as the author of this work.

British Library Cataloguing in Publication Data:
A catalogue record for this book is available from the British Library

ISBN(13) 978-1-903065-95-2 Illustrations copyright © 2022 Jan Budkowski, Adobe Stock Images and others Typesetting by Zambezi Publishing Ltd, Plymouth

All rights reserved. No part of this publication may be reproduced, stored in a retrieval system, or transmitted in any form or by any means, electronic, mechanical, photocopying, recording or otherwise, whether currently existing or yet to be developed, without the prior written permission of the publisher.
This book is sold subject to the condition that it shall not, by way of trade or otherwise, be lent, resold, hired out or otherwise circulated without the publisher's prior written consent, in any form of binding, cover or format other than that in which it is originally published, and without a similar condition being imposed
on the subsequent purchaser.

Disclaimer:- This book is intended to provide general information regarding the subject matter, and to entertain. The contents are not exhaustive and no warranty is given as to accuracy of content. The book is sold on the understanding that neither the publisher nor the author are thereby engaged in rendering professional services, in respect of the subject matter or any other field. If expert guidance is required, the services of a qualified professional should be sought. Readers are urged to access a range of other material on the book's subject matter, and to tailor the information to their individual needs. Neither the author nor the publisher shall have any responsibility to any person or entity regarding any loss or damage caused or alleged to be caused, directly or indirectly, by the use or misuse of information contained in this book. If you do not wish to be bound by the above, you may return this book in original condition to the publisher, with its receipt, for a refund of the purchase price.

About the Author

Sasha turned a childhood interest in palmistry and astrology into a career when she was in her twenties, later adding Tarot and developing her psychic abilities. She worked as a professional consultant from 1974 onwards, learning her trade in the best way possible - by doing readings for clients. She reduced her workload when her writing career took off, and over the past twenty-five years has mainly concentrated on writing and publishing, but she still does the occasional professional reading to keep her skills relevant.

At present, Sasha's tally is 140 books, published by a number of mainstream publishers around the world. This now includes her three Tudorland novels.

Sasha wrote the stars page for Woman's Own magazine for six years and for the Sunday People's Weekend Magazine for a couple of years before that. She wrote a syndicated column for many local papers and about 3,000 articles and columns for papers and magazines of all kinds, mainly for the UK market but some for Australia.

Sasha has broadcast on many BBC and independent radio stations in the UK, with several regular spots that carried on for many years. She had her own spot on United Artists television for five years. Sasha now broadcasts from time to time on internet radio stations and podcasts around the world.

Sasha has given talks and workshops at hundreds of festivals in the UK and overseas, including the large Mind, Body and Spirit festivals in London and Australia.

Posts held:
Former President of the British Astrological and Psychic Society (BAPS)
Former Chair of the Advisory Panel on Astrological Education (APAE)
Former member of the Executive Council of the Writers' Guild of Great Britain

Sasha and her husband, Jan Budkowski, opened Zambezi Publishing in November 1996 and have since published over 300 books as an independent publisher. Most of their work is now co-editions and packaging projects. They have worked with Sterling Publishing Inc, Red Wheel Weiser, Charlesbridge, Parragon, Welbeck and Quarto.

Contents

Introduction 9
1: The Solar System 17
2: The Sun 25
3: Mercury 31
4: Venus 41
5: Mars 49
6: Jupiter 59
7: Saturn 77
8: Uranus 91
9: Neptune 101
10: Pluto 111
11: Chiron 119
12: Planetary Cycles Table 125
Conclusion 133
Index 135

Introduction

You Don't Need to be an Astrologer

The planets orbit the solar system, with each making a complete circuit of the Sun at one time or another, and these circuits affect every one of us at various points in our lives. The good news is that you don't need to be an astrologer to understand and use planetary cycles, and you don't need a birth chart or specialised software either. Working by hand is fine at first, but it will lack precision and accuracy where the distant planets are concerned, so it won't be totally accurate when you look at older age groups. You might have to jiggle the timelines forward and backwards by a few years when it comes to checking out senior citizens.

If you are getting into astrology, you can buy an astrology app for your smartphone for about £10 or so. I have a little app on my mobile phone that shows charts and lists of planets, and even a description of how each planet affects us, so I find it useful when I'm on the move. However, there is nothing like decent software, and the best programs I know of are Solar Fire or Winstar. Some other programs may look good, but not all of them work properly. Don't just go for the cheapest item, but on the other hand, you don't need the most expensive versions unless you are definitely aiming to become a professional astrologer.

You might want to buy some paper ephemerides books for the 20th century and the first half of the 21st century. My favourite ephemeris is "The Astrolabe World Ephemeris 2001-2050 at Midnight", published by Schiffer Publishing Ltd. I always buy the annual Raphael's ephemeris as well, because I find it handy for checking out the planets on any day in the current year.

Introduction

Note for Astrologers
Because this book is aimed at anyone vaguely interested in astrology, whether they know much about it or not, I have tried to be consistent in my use of the terms *returns*, *half-returns* and *quarter-returns*. The moment one gets into astrology, one discovers that these aspects are better known as *conjunctions*, *oppositions* and *squares*, so I also use those terms in this book.

Planetary Cycles by Age Groups
The following table will show you the times when changes will occur. You will learn about these and others in detail in this book, but you may find this table handy to refer to or to check up on from time to time. At the end of the book, I repeat this table, so it will make even more sense to you when you have reached that point.

Key to Code
    R   Return
    HR   Half-Return
    QR   Quarter-Return
    ER   Eighth-Return

Astrological Cycles In Focus

Ages	Planets	Brief Interpretations
6	Jupiter HR	Education and sports or activities become important now. End of babyhood.
7 – 8	Saturn QR	Can bring major problems, especially concerning the child's father.
11 – 12	Jupiter R	Changes of school, fairly happy time, success and achievement, making new friends.
12 – 13	Chiron QR	Education and sport are important, some unhappiness.
14 – 15	Saturn HR	Growing up, puberty, becoming responsible for self.
18 – 19	Jupiter HR	Problems in education or love life but soon overcome.
20 – 21	Uranus QR	Big change, education, love, pregnancy, job improvement.
20 – 21	Neptune ER	Falling in love, pregnancy, happy time.
24 – 25	Jupiter R	Should be happy, successful time for career and personal life. May travel a bit now.
25 – 26	Chiron HR	Realisation that something needs to change, could be training for a better job.
29	Saturn R	Major turning point for good after difficult time. Growing up, parenthood, responsibility, work changes.
30	Jupiter HR	Coming to terms with changes going on. Productive time.

Introduction

Ages	Planets	Brief Interpretations
36	Jupiter R	Major decisions, often related to childbirth.
38 – 39	Chiron QR	Irritating time when problems start to surface.
39 – 40	Uranus HR	Major change of direction.
41 – 42	Neptune QR	A stressful time at home or work. Health may be a problem.
42	Jupiter HR	Money may be a problem, or luck may be against the person.
40 – 45	Pluto QR	A time of transformation, which could go in any direction, but comes right after a period of difficulty.
44 – 45	Saturn HR	A heavy responsibility lands on the person. Must face up to reality.
48	Jupiter R	A time of happiness, expansion and something new which could be very successful.
50 – 52	Chiron R	A difficult time for health, accidents and trouble in love life and personal relationships. Change of life for women.
54	Jupiter HR	A somewhat tricky time when travel and foreigners could cause problems. Health may be a problem.
56 – 58	Saturn R	A time of realisation that things must change. Maybe retirement, something new, reward for effort but also sadness as things come to an end.
60	Jupiter R	A good time with more spirituality, travel perhaps, fun and joy.

Astrological Cycles In Focus

Ages	Planets	Brief Interpretations
62 – 63	Neptune ER	Spirituality develops, people show kindness, but muddles and even swindles can occur behind the person's back.
63	Uranus QR	A battle may need to be fought and a new attitude taken. Something must change.
63 – 64	Chiron QR	Health may be a problem now, and the subject needs to get a grip in many areas of life.
66	Jupiter HR	A time to face up to the need for change and a new direction.
72	Jupiter R	A productive time with new interests and a measure of success. Some travel or foreign friendships.
72	Saturn HR	Facing up to reality, maybe move of house or other practical matters.
76 – 77	Chiron HR	Health may be a problem now.
78	Jupiter HR	Financial setback, or trouble connected to spiritual matters or foreigners.
82 – 83	Neptune HR	An unexpected and possibly unusual health problem.
84	Jupiter R	Time of success and achievement.
84	Uranus R	Sudden changes; could be very good but unsettling.
87 – 88	Saturn R	Facing up to some form of reality.

Introduction

AGES	PLANETS	BRIEF INTERPRETATIONS
88 – 90	Chiron QR	Health issues and some sadness or loss.
96	Jupiter HR	Loss of some measure of independence, restriction.
102 – 103	Neptune ER	Spiritual matters become important, may pass over now.
108	Jupiter R	Drawing to the end of a long and interesting life, very interested in spiritual matters.

1: The Solar System

Astronomy

For the moment, let us look at the planets as though we were astronomers rather than as astrologers. We know that the planets orbit the Sun, and we also know that our earth is one of the planets in the solar system.

The following table shows the average length of time that it takes each planet to orbit the Sun. The planets orbit the Sun in an elliptical fashion rather than in a circle, which means that there are times when they are closer to the Sun and apparently travelling faster than usual, and times when they are distant from the Sun and apparently, moving more slowly, so this makes the planetary orbits vary from one time to another.

1: The Solar System

PLANET	ORBIT
Mercury	3 Earth months.
Venus	7 Earth months.
Earth	1 Earth year. (365.25 days)
Mars	23 Earth months. Almost 2 Earth years.
Jupiter	42 Earth months. Almost 12 Earth years.
Saturn	354 Earth months. (29.5 Earth years)
Uranus	1009 Earth months. (84 Earth years)
Neptune	1979 Earth months. (Almost 165 Earth years)
Pluto	2977 Earth months. (248 Earth years)
Chiron	612 Earth months (51 Earth years)

No Time of Birth?
Most astrology readings require a full horoscope, constructed from the date, time and place of birth, but fortunately, planetary cycles will work for everybody, including those who don't know their time of birth! However, it is always best to have the full birth data if possible.

The Sun, Earth and the Ecliptic
Astrology is "geocentric", which means that we look at the solar system from our standpoint on Earth, as though the

Astrological Cycles In Focus

Sun and all the other planets were orbiting us on Earth. Ancient astronomers and astrologers thought the Sun orbited the earth, and astronomers still use the apparent path of the Sun as a way of finding their way around the sky. This apparent trajectory is called the *ecliptic* or more commonly, *the zodiac*, and the twelve signs of the zodiac line up along

the ecliptic. The ecliptic is very important to astrologers because everything in astrology happens along it.

1: The Solar System

Returns and Half-Returns

The transits that matter in planetary cycles are returns - which are also conjunctions and half-returns - which are also oppositions.

Returns

A very simple return that we all know is our birthday, because this is when the Sun returns to the place it occupied when we were born. So, this may be where the expression "many happy returns" comes from.

Lunar returns occur much more frequently, as it only takes an average of 28 days for the Moon to make each lunar return.

Half-Returns and Other Transits

- Half-returns occur when a planet is halfway around its orbit and is therefore opposite its natal position. This is more commonly known as an opposition.
- Quarter-returns occur when a planet is a quarter of the way around its orbit and is therefore in a square aspect to its natal position.
- Sextiles occur when the planet is two signs away from its original position.
- Trines occur when the planet is four signs away.
- Inconjuncts occur when a planet is five signs away.
- Semi-sextiles occur when a planet is one sign away.
- Semi-squares occur when a planet is 45 degrees away.
- Quintiles occur when a planet is 72 degrees away.

Orbs

Orbs are the distance between planets when they make an aspect. Astrologers have different views about the orbs they like to use, but most would agree with an orb of eight degrees for a conjunction or opposition, while some prefer

Astrological Cycles In Focus

an orb of ten degrees. Six degrees will do for most other aspects, with minor aspects and minor features on a birth chart only needing one or two degrees at most.

A planetary transit will make itself felt in the run-up to the actual aspect, and when it reaches exactitude and starts to separate, the event fades fairly quickly. However, the change that it precipitates can have a lingering effect.

Retrograde Motion

Sometimes the planets appear to be travelling backwards in the sky, and this is known as retrograde motion. It happens when the Earth appears to be moving more quickly than the planet. Mercury will usually turn retrograde three times in a year, while Venus and Mars do so every couple of years or so. The outer planets appear to be retrograde for a few weeks when the Sun is on the other side of the chart to them. For instance, if the outer planets are in Capricorn and the Sun is travelling through part of Taurus, Gemini, Cancer, Leo and part of Virgo, the planet in Capricorn will be retrograde.

The nodes of the Moon are always retrograde.

Elliptical Orbits

As I said earlier, planetary orbits are not circular but somewhat elongated, so there are times when they are closer to the Sun (perihelion), which makes them move through the signs of the zodiac more quickly than normal. There are times when they are further away from the Sun (aphelion), which means they take longer to move through the zodiac. The main effect of this deviation is seen in the outer planets.

The first Saturn return should occur at the age of 29.5, but for those born in the 20th century, it can be felt at the age of 28, and its effect is usually in full flood by 29.

1: The Solar System

The second Saturn return should occur at the age of 59, but it can turn up earlier, at anything from 56 to 58.

The Uranus half-return should occur at the age of 42, but for the generation alive now, the Uranus half-return occurs at about the age of 39 to 40.

The Chiron return has been running somewhat slowly, and it tended to affect people around the age of 51 to 52, but it must be speeding up now, because I notice those at the age of 49 to 50 experiencing Chiron events.

The outer planets of Neptune and Pluto won't make a return in a subject's lifetime, but the half-returns and quarter-returns are important, but the orbits are so irregular that the only way of finding these transits is by using quality software or an ephemeris.

Astrologers have only recently started to work with the asteroids, but there is information in some ephemerides and in good software.

The Moon

The Moon orbits the earth every 27.32 earth days. Your software will have no problem dealing with this calculation, but astrologers tend to use a quick-fix guide of 28 days.

Distant Planets

New planets are being discovered all the time, and some astrologers note how they affect us. For instance, you may find it interesting to see that Eris has a 500-year orbit, and it is now back where it was at the time of the Reformation. The 16th and 17th-century religious wars tore Europe apart and reduced its population by half in some areas, so it will be interesting to see what this transit brings.

2: The Sun

THE SUN

Orbit: *365.25 days.*
Symbolism: *Apollo, god of healing, light and music.*

Solar Returns and Half-Returns

The Sun is a star, but astrologers call everything a planet for the sake of simplicity. The Sun is a personal planet because it is not far from the Earth.

The one planetary return that we all know very well is the solar return, because that is when the Sun returns to the exact place that it was when we were born, and of course, this is our birthday. There is a solar return every year, and a half-return occurs when the Sun is on the other side of the astrology chart and, therefore, opposite the natal Sun. So, for instance, if you were born on the 10th of September, the solar return would occur on the 10th of September each year, and the half return or opposition would occur on the 10th of March each year.

The solar return is usually a happy time, with birthday celebrations. Still, those who are old and very ill often die around the time of their birthday, because it seems that the energy released by having the Sun so close to its original natal position starts the sick person's journey to the other side. Quarter-returns (square aspects) to the Sun occur three months and nine months after each solar return when the Sun is 90 degrees away from its natal position.

The first quarter-return could be a slightly tense time, when a problem starts to show up.

The half-return is usually difficult, either due to a health problem such as a bad cold, or perhaps a time when dealing with other people is difficult.

2: The Sun

The third quarter-return is a tense time as this brings the problem that started with the first quarter-return to a head, which allows it to be cleared up.

Things Associated with the Sun

Sign of the Zodiac:
Leo.

Winning, Achieving, Succeeding
The Sun is a planet of success and achievement.

Creativity
All forms of creativity or manifestation are the province of the Sun.

Children
The children we create are signified by the Sun and the sign it is in on our birth chart. Children in general, and the games and fun we have with them, are partly ruled by the Sun and partly by Mercury.

Fathers and Father Figures
This aspect of astrology has become somewhat forgotten, but it used to be the case that the Moon ruled the mother, and the Sun ruled the father. In my opinion, this still applies, although I also look at Saturn to represent the authority figure that is often also the father.

Business
Success and enjoyment engendered by a business belong to the Sun, while it also rules glamorous businesses and ones that give pleasure to others.

Astrological Cycles In Focus

Time Off
Entertainments, parties, holidays, nights out, visiting a casino or a racetrack, playing games and having fun.

Music
All kinds of music and the pleasure we get from it are ruled by the Sun.

Love Affairs
Flirting, casual love affairs, outings with a lover, or outings with good friends and having fun all apply, but not long-term relationships.

Metal
Gold.

Health and Healing
The Sun rules the spine and the heart.

Random Items
Jewellery, glitter, happiness.

Extra Notes
Retrograde Motion
The Sun doesn't turn to retrograde motion.

The Signs and Houses
Check out the signs and houses to see how the Sun activates them when it passes through them.

A Solar Return Chart
It can be interesting to look at a solar return chart, which puts the Sun back to its position at your time and date of

2: The Sun

birth. The most important thing to look at here is the ascendant, as it seems to offer a flavour of the coming year.

Sample Charts
Sylvester Stallone
The following two charts are Sylvester Stallone's natal chart and his solar return chart for 2021, which I have set for Los Angeles, assuming that this is his current home. The ascendant for the natal chart is at the very end of Sagittarius, so most of his natal first house is in Capricorn, suggesting a difficult childhood and a lot of hard work until he was at least into his mid-thirties. The solar return ascendant for this year will be early in the sign of Capricorn.

The solar return ascendant could be in any sign, but by chance, it happens to be close to his birth ascendant this time round, so it seems that he will revisit some of the struggles he went through early in his life, or there could be a time of hard work to come.

There is much more to say about this solar return chart, but I will leave it at that for now.

If you want to set up the natal and solar return charts for Sylvester Stallone and view the details for yourself, his birth data is below. Interestingly, his mother is an astrologer!

Birth Data: 6 July 1946 at 19:20 in New York, USA

Sylvester was born on a Saturday, which traditionally foretells a difficult start in life and a lot of hard work leading to eventual success.

As it happens, Sylvester has the Sun in Cancer in the seventh house, so I expect he likes to celebrate his birthday traditionally with family and friends around him. The solar half-return occurs on the 6th of January and is in Capricorn in his first house, so maybe work or plans for the kind of publicity that will enhance his reputation have to take place

Astrological Cycles In Focus

at that time. He might find this arduous, as his health won't be at its best at the half-return, but it must be done. He was born with some facial damage and a difficult start in life. Still, he worked his way out of his problems and went on to have a very successful life, shown by his Jupiter conjunct his midheaven in the cardinal sign of Libra.

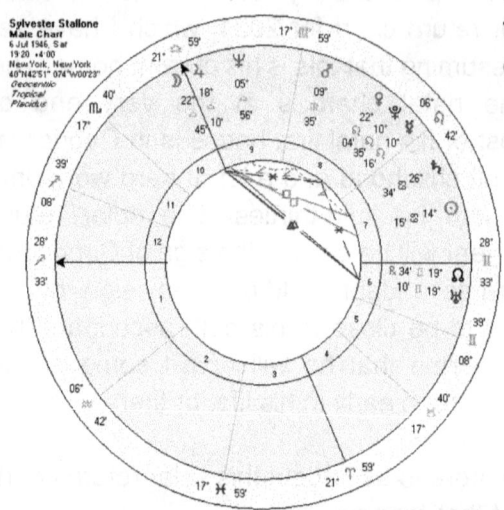

Silvester Stallone - natal chart

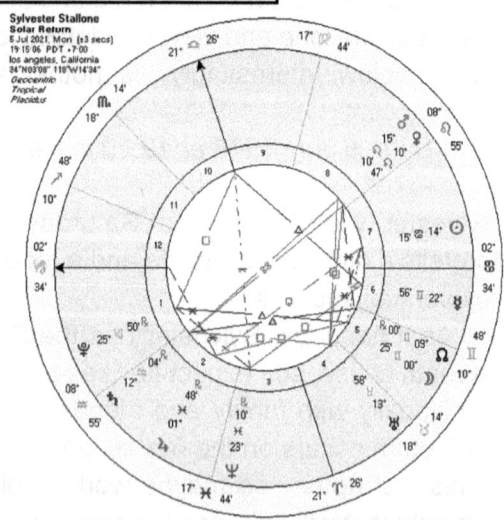

Silvester Stallone - Solar Return chart

3: Mercury

Mercury

Orbit: *87.97 days.*
Symbolic ideas: *The messenger and the god of healing.*

Mercury is called a personal planet because it is not far from the earth.

The returns of Mercury don't usually make a great impact on your life, so you may not even notice them, but if you happen to have a return, half-return or even a quarter-return coming up, watch what happens. Mercury moves so quickly that it relates to daily-life situations rather than major events. You might notice something happening in your working life, but a Mercury half-return or quarter-return could register a minor inconvenience.

The return should be good, or at the very least, it will bring something to your attention so you can deal with it.

The half-return will be awkward, with people letting you down and being unhelpful, or something may break down just when you most need it.

The quarter-return can be tricky, with the first square setting off a problem and the last one helping you to find a way of solving it.

Now you can look up the concepts associated with Mercury, and you will be surprised at how many possibilities there are.

Things Associated With Mercury

Signs of the Zodiac
Gemini and Virgo. Virgo can also be linked to the dwarf planet, Chiron.

3: Mercury

Young People
Traditionally speaking, Mercury is a neutral planet, so its energy isn't specifically male or female, but it does link with youth and youthfulness.

Orphans
A link exists between Mercury and those who were orphaned, given up for adoption, or felt out of step with their family or schoolmates while growing up. The outcome is that these people learn to rely on themselves rather than others and to think for themselves, thus making them more independent.

Basic Education
This might be primary or secondary education, but it is not usually associated with higher education. It could relate to job training, especially if it involves communication, using a computer or getting around. So, Mercury would come into play if you were learning to drive a lorry, taking the driving test, or training for a job.

Communication
Some people find it easy to communicate while others struggle with this, and it is worth checking out their Mercury on a natal chart to see whether it is in good condition or not. Mercury relates to language, possibly learning a foreign language or dealing with people whose first language is not English. This planet rules intellect, logic, ability to reason and to write. It rules the type of mentality a person has. It also links with telephones, texts, emails, snail mail or mail shots. It rules the local newspaper, local radio and television and the postman. Advertising and marketing are Mercurial activities.

Speech
Mercury rules the way we speak, so when Mercury runs opposite (half-return) or square (quarter-return) to its natal position, it's best to watch what we say, write or email to others.

Movement
Traditionally, Mercury is associated with travel and transport of a relatively local kind instead of long-distance travel. However, when you go back a century or so, people hardly left their own villages. These days, we routinely travel long distances for business or pleasure, so it's hard to differentiate between these types of travel. Local travel includes buses, taxis, trains, bicycles, vehicles of any kind and even walking to work.

Neighbourhood
Mercury rules local matters, the area you live and work in, the neighbours, running local errands, taking the children to the local park and so on.

Relationships
Mercury is concerned with brothers, sisters and relationships of that kind, so cousins and other relatives of one's generation fall into this category, along with friendships that feel like brother/sister relationships. It also denotes neighbours and other people who we deal with in our locality.

Metal
Mercury, quicksilver.

3: Mercury

Youth
Mercury is a planet associated with youth, so while it doesn't rule our relationship with our own children, it is associated with teaching young people or such things as playgroups, pre-schools, dancing schools, drama clubs, scouts, guides, cubs, brownies, cadets, outdoor activities and anything else related to children and young people.

Health and Healing
There is an ancient Greek myth that Mercury was walking down the street when he saw two snakes fighting; while they took a break to draw back and hiss at each other for a while, Mercury threw down his staff between the two snakes. The snakes wound their way round the staff, which promptly grew wings at the top to mimic the small wings on Mercury's feet, and this became the Caduceus, or the symbol of healing.

Even astrologers tend to forget Mercury's connection to health and healing. They seem to blank out that this small planet is linked to medical work, whether conventional, complementary or alternative. Being so concerned with communication, it is to some extent also linked to psychology and psychotherapy. The main health areas are the shoulders, arms, wrists and hands, and accidents or damage to these body parts. Mercury also rules the bronchial tubes, the brain, the tip of the tongue and the nervous system. It is strongly linked to colds, flu, bronchial infections and so on.

Masters and Servants
The old idea was that Mercury ruled masters and servants, but today this means staff and employers, but the planet also rules work. It is especially associated with jobs that involve communication, journalism and writing, but it is also

connected with maths in the form of accountancy and, to some extent, the donkey work associated with banking. It rules craftsmanship, making things and using our hands so that it can connect to blueprints and engineering design.

Business and Contracts
Mercury is associated with trade and commerce, also with using technical skills for work purposes. I have noticed over the years that Jan and I tend to sign important contracts or buy expensive office equipment whenever Mercury is retrograde. There is no astrological sense to this, but it is a fact.

Magic
Mercury is also associated with magic, which covers both magic as entertainment, card tricks and sawing the lady in half, and real magic with rituals and spell casting, Wicca, traditional witchcraft, and so on.

Theft and Trickery
Mercury was a trickster god in mythology, so this planet is associated with confidence tricks, thieves and thieving; everything from car theft, mugging, house breaking and embezzlement to petty theft.

Emotional Effect
Mercury is not supposed to be linked to emotion, because it suggests intellectual activity rather than emotional responses. However, there is a world of difference between astrological theory and reality. The main emotion associated with Mercury is worry, and it can lead to anything from mild stress, depression and discontent to abnormal levels of neurosis. At best, a Mercury half or quarter-return could set off a short period of worry, or it could bring on a minor infection. However, we might say the wrong thing to the wrong person, or

3: Mercury

something upsetting could happen to us at work. Mercury can bring success and happiness when in a good aspect to itself, or an upsetting time when it is a challenging aspect. Mercury can set people off on a phase of complaining, grizzling, belly aching, moaning, groaning and feeling sorry for themselves.

Other Random Connections
Mercury is linked to termini, so using railway hubs, airports, car hire and all manner of starting and ending points for journeys can be affected by Mercury cycles on your chart. Also cinnabar and yellow gems, such as citrine.

Dan's story
Dan is an electrician, and he drives his van from place to place for his job. I always warn him whenever Mercury turns retrograde because that's when something is likely to go wrong, and he often tells me that there are more bad drivers than usual on the roads at that time and that some of his jobs turn out to be more difficult than usual. On the last retrograde Mercury, Dan was driving carefully through the London rush hour when a duck ran out in front of his van and stood stock-still in the middle of the road! He said, if he hadn't known Mercury was retrograde and hadn't been driving slowly and keeping his eyes peeled, he could easily have had a nasty accident, and the duck would have been history!

Extra Notes

The Signs and Houses
The way that a Mercury cycle will play out depends upon whether it is close to an angle or a planet, or which houses are activated by the cycle. For example, a Mercury half-return where the natal Mercury is in the second house and the half-return is coming at it from the

eighth house could bring unexpected expense, especially where officialdom is concerned.

A Sample Chart
Pamela Anderson
Birth data: 1 July 1967 at 4:08 in Ladysmith, Canada

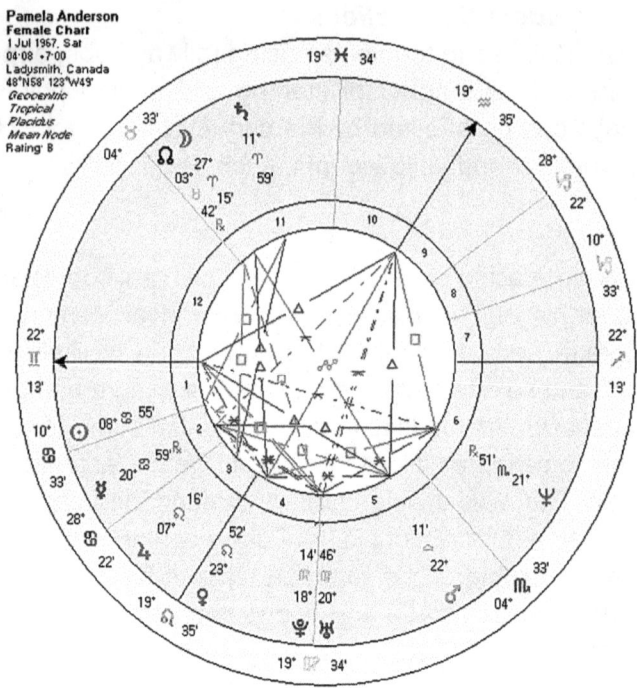

The gorgeous Pamela Anderson is a Marilyn Monroe figure, as she had a spectacular career, mainly built around her beauty and her ability to work on screen and television. Whereas Marilyn had the Sun in Gemini, Pamela has the Sun in Cancer, but she has Gemini rising.

Gemini rising is never an easy ascendant to grow up with, and needless to say, little Pamela's parents didn't protect her. Being a pretty little girl, she attracted sexual

3: Mercury

abuse from the age of four onwards from both men and women, including being gang-raped by her then-boyfriend and his pals at the age of fourteen. Mercury is her ruling planet, but it is retrograde and in the second house, so I guess that she has made good money throughout her life and probably had a good business head on her shoulders due to her Sun in the shrewd sign of Cancer and her Mercury in the second house of personal finances.

However, her Mercury is retrograde, so she must have heard many lies from the men who latched on to her, and she must have been desperate to believe them. If you check out her work record on Wikipedia, she has clearly worked herself into the ground to keep herself, her children and the stream of husbands and boyfriends. Her Mercury is trine to Neptune, which is good for a film career, and Neptune is the god who rules the sea, so it isn't surprising that she found fame with Baywatch. She has written a couple of books and became politically active in later life, fighting for several good causes.

Mercury moves too quickly to check for life cycles, but it is likely that every time it squares or opposes that retrograde natal Mercury, it brings arguments and aggravation at work, in her personal life, in business, politically and via the media.

4: Venus

VENUS

Orbit: *224.65 days.*
Symbolic ideas: *The bringer of harmony and peace.*

Venus is called a personal planet because it is not far from the Earth.

The returns of Venus are frequent, so you may not notice them, but if you happen to have a return, half-return or even a quarter-return coming up, watch to see what happens and judge for yourself whether it has any recognisable effect. As with all transits, there is always tension during the run-up to the event, which fades quickly once the transit has passed. Venus aspects are likely to set off something pleasant, such as a good night out, a shopping trip, lovemaking and happy times. Half-returns and squares can set off arguments, disappointments in your love life, minor losses or something as upsetting as a visit to the hairdresser that leaves you with a big bill and a bad hairdo.

The return should be good, so your social life, and dealings with women will be successful for a while.

The half-return will be awkward, with people (especially women) letting you down or being unwilling to help you, or maybe you buy something that costs more than expected.

The quarter-return can be tricky, with the first square setting off a problem and the last one making you find a way to solve it.

Now you can look up the many things associated with Venus, and you will be surprised at how many possibilities there are.

4: Venus

Things Associated with Venus

Signs of the Zodiac
Taurus and Libra. Libra could also be linked to the asteroid Ceres.

Balance and Harmony
Things that are working well and are in balance rather than out of gear in some way.

Values and Priorities
The things you value, such as behaving in the right way, honesty, kindness, preserving the Earth, being a good homemaker, making money, or many other matters.

Personal Finances
This is not what your business is worth or even what your partner has; it is what you are worth in terms of your estate.

Valuable Goods and Personal Possessions
Things that are important to you. These could be anything at all, from a car, an Xbox, furniture, jewellery or ornaments that once belonged to much-loved family members. For example, I have two pewter elephants that are worthless in monetary terms, but they belonged to my step-Grandfather, who lived in Southern Africa in the early days of those countries, and I loved listening to him talk about his adventures. Much later in my life, I was offered an opportunity to go to Southern Africa and I jumped at it, partly inspired by Grandfather and the elephants.

Partners
The position of Venus in the natal chart shows the kind of partner that the person finds attractive. In other

circumstances, Venus can show the kind of people that we like as friends, along with the Moon and other factors on a chart. It also shows whether we are choosy or not.

Relationships
Venus was associated with marriage in days gone by, but now it connects with partnerships and relationships of all kinds. It is particularly concerned with happy relationships.

Love, Romance and Sex
The ability to love and relate to others, attraction, sexuality, relationships and the happiness involved in a great love life. Believe it or not, Venus is the goddess that links with aphrodisiacs and even with venereal disease! Well, let's hope those who suffer from it did so in the pursuit of pleasure!

Open Enemies
Just as Venus rules open love relationships and deep friendships, it also rules open enemies. It isn't linked to the kind of person who is nice to your face but who stabs you in the back but someone who is openly opposed to you. The position of Venus on a chart may also show the reason for this.

Leisure and Pleasure
A great meal out, a holiday in a good hotel, a weekend of pampering in a spa. Anything that involves luxury and makes you feel like a prince or princess for a while comes into this category. This could include outright ostentation in some circumstances.

Music and Art
Anything that gives you artistic pleasure comes into this category, so it could be a lovely picture, watching Strictly Come Dancing on the television or going to a rock concert and singing along to the music.

4: Venus

Metal
Copper, and because mirrors used to be made of copper, Venus rules mirrors.

Health
Venus rules the throat, lower jaw and neck. It also rules the pancreas, kidneys, bladder and the ability to move about and walk. It is often associated with diabetes.

Legal Matters, Arbitration and Justice
There is a connection to the law here, but also to links between people for legal or business purposes, such as Trades Unions, arbitration, courts, and such things as employment agencies, literary or entertainment business agencies and so on. I short, those who try to get a fair deal for all parties while earning a commission for themselves.

Emotional Effect
Emotions connected with love, passion, sex, personal possessions and finances.

Other Random Connections
Cosmetics and the cosmetic industry, powder compacts, mirrors, seashells, flowers, oysters, malachite, emeralds, and of course, Venetian blinds.

Extra Notes

Venus Retrograde
When Venus is retrograde, life is grey, cold, short of fun and boring. Financial or legal affairs may be delayed, or they may not go well. Love and marriage may not be enjoyable, and friends may not be kind or friendly. It isn't a good time to spend money on luxury goods or

Astrological Cycles In Focus

lash out on an expensive, luxury holiday because it would be disappointing.

The Signs and Houses

The way that a Venus cycle will play out depends upon whether it is close to an angle or a planet, or which houses are activated by the cycle. For example, a Venus half-return where the natal Venus is in the fourth house and the half-return is coming at it from the tenth house could make it hard to cope with the demands of home and career at the same time, and your life could be out of balance in some way for a few months. You need to check out the chapter on the signs and houses to make sense of these cycles.

A Sample Chart
Barbara Castle

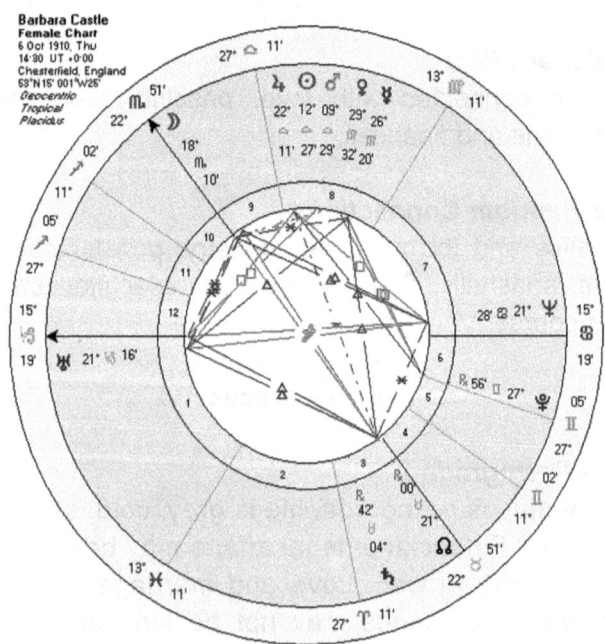

Barbara Castle - Natal chart

4: Venus

Barbara was one of the most effective MPs in the Labour party during the 1960s and one of the few women to get anywhere in those early days. She had a good childhood with a hard-working family who were politically active, and both her siblings went into variations of political life. Her Capricorn ascendant shows that her family taught her the value of hard work. Capricorn can be linked to poverty in some way, and Barbara's mother once ran a soup kitchen for out of work miners.

She was small and pretty with lovely red hair, and she was also highly intelligent. She was later called the Maggie Thatcher of the Labour party. Unsurprisingly, her birthday is similar to Margaret Thatcher's, as both were Librans and both came from similar family backgrounds. During World War Two, Barbara worked at the Ministry of Food (interestingly, both Virgo and Libra are often connected to food) and she had planets in both Virgo and Libra. Her greatest claim to parliamentary fame was as the Secretary of State for Employment from 1968 to 1970, but a combination of a bad time for industry, too much power in the hands of the trades unions and back-stabbers in parliament, brought her career to an end, after which she sat in the House of Lords for a few years.

With a strong Venus, being the ruler of her Sun sign and high on her chart in the ninth house, it is likely that she would have prospered during good Venus aspects and suffered setbacks on the challenging ones or whenever Venus turned to retrograde motion.

5: Mars

MARS

Orbit: *1 year and 320 days.*
Symbolic ideas: *The bringer of war.*
Mars is called a personal planet because within the solar system, it is relatively speaking not far from the earth.

The orbit of Mars around the Sun takes almost two earth years, which makes its returns, half-returns and other cycles much more noticeable than those of Mercury and Venus. In theory, the nature of Mars means that it makes us fight, or perhaps we will find ourselves in a passionate embrace. Well, that's the theory...

In ancient times before telescopes were invented, astrologers called Mars and Saturn "the great malefics", and even today, new students quickly learn to dislike Saturn, but it doesn't occur to them to worry about Mars. Frankly, I am far more wary of Mars than I am of Saturn, because I know from experience that something will upset me when a Mars cycle activates itself on my chart, or I might fall ill or have an accident. The actual return should bring good times, but it can still throw up a few unpleasant surprises or a mixture of good and bad incidents simultaneously.

Fortunately, the effects of the returns only last for two or three weeks, so they aren't life-changing, but Mars is a powerful planet that can't be ignored, and its effect can be felt even as the transit fades. If a return or a transit to a sensitive spot on your chart happens while Mars turns from direct to retrograde motion, stands still for a while and finally turns back to direct motion, it will take several

5: Mars

months to clear, and it will be memorable. However, this is a rare occurrence.

It is worth checking the houses involved, as that will give some idea of how an event might play out. For instance, a Mars return in the first house may bring a visit to the dentist, because the first house is about you and the body.

If the Mars return occurs in the eighth house and a personal relationship makes you unhappy, something will bring things to a head, so this could easily be the last straw that breaks the camel's back. This is even more likely during the half-return when the transiting Mars is opposite your natal Mars. If your natal Mars happened to be in the second house and the half-return happens in the eighth house, and you are coming to a parting of the ways, it is likely to be a costly event since money and possessions will be involved at both ends of the half-return.

Another point to consider is the signs involved, because a natal Mars in the earth sign of Taurus is not going to be half as lively as one in a fire sign or even an air sign. In fire signs (Aries, Leo and Sagittarius), the Mars return, half-return, or even the square can set off a short-term conflagration, so always make a mental note of the signs and houses involved.

* * *

The Mars myth is of a young warrior who sets out to fight the foe with his sister Eris, so Mars suggests courage, assertion, confidence, and a strong survival instinct. A Mars return is likely to kick-start an eventuality that requires courage, heart and the ability to fight for what you want. This may not be a bad thing, but it will certainly put your courage to the test. For instance, in a working situation, you might be asked to do something that takes you out of your comfort zone; you may be offered the kind of promotion that involves taking on much more responsibility, or you may find yourself in competition with someone else. You may decide to start a business of your own. Whatever you choose to do should work out well, but it will definitely take some doing. Mars rules courage, determination and moving at speed, so whatever happens, there will be no time to ponder the implications.

Mars rules competing, so it could mean being involved in sports or supporting a team, but many situations make people competitive. For instance, you may be encouraged to compete against others to be the greatest salesperson at your place of work, or you may wish to become the chair of a committee ahead of others who you feel are less able to do the job. Rivalry in families, friends and even neighbours is common, and a Mars event can rev up all these issues.

There is a military aspect to Mars, so you might become a part-time soldier, a community police officer or a leader in some youth organisation. You may teach team-building among the young or organise paintball outings as team building jaunts for businesspeople.

Mars is a masculine influence, strongly associated with passion and sex, so it may bring exciting affairs your way. It may register the kind of passion that overwhelms everyone at the start of a new love affair, but whether this will turn into lasting love is another matter, because that is the province of Venus rather than Mars. So, the passion that is involved might include love and affection or it might not. Also, Mars being what it is, the whole episode might not last long.

The passion you feel might not be for love and sex at all but for something else, which could be anything from politics to sports, a hobby and much else. I have a friend who loves steam railways, so a pleasant Mars aspect, such as a return, sextile or trine, would send him off for a few days of joyful steam-trainspotting. This makes sense because Mars is associated with fire and iron, so it would be a perfect Mars activity. Motor racing is another typical Martian activity because it involves speed, heat, metal and courage. In theory, a sporting event should work out well if Mars is on a return, sextile or trine, but it will probably be disappointing if it is on a quarter or a half-return. Most of us like watching competitions, hence the huge following for Strictly Come Dancing or The X Factor. Healthy competition is the province of Mars.

If you are a woman experiencing a Mars return, a young man may make an appearance in your life, but the role he plays and whether he stays around or not depend upon a host of other things on your chart. A Mars square or opposition might bring an argument or even a physical attack your way, so take care who you mix with and where you go. If it is a woman who is playing a part in your life at the moment, she will be dynamic with a steamroller personality, and she may overwhelm you. You may remember a song called Jolene which Dolly Parton used to sing, in which she begged Jolene not to take her man just because she could. So, when dynamic women and Mars are around, take care not to allow some other woman to take over your home, your job, your business interests or your man, just because she has an excess of energy and drive that she could use for the purpose.

Another possibility is that someone may come into your life for a while who has the Sun, Moon or Ascendant in Aries or the first house.

Here are a few more ideas associated with Mars:
- The return should be good, so your working life, social life and dealings with men should be successful for a while.
- The half-return will be awkward, and people may behave in an unpleasantly aggressive manner towards you.

Astrological Cycles In Focus

- The quarter-return can be tricky, with the first square setting off a problem and the last one forcing you to find a way of solving it.

Now you can look up the many things associated with Mars, and you will be surprised at how many possibilities there are.

Things Associated with Mars

Signs of the Zodiac
Aries. In ancient astrology, Mars also ruled Scorpio.

Decisiveness
Taking charge, decision making, activity and action of all kinds.

Types of Occupation
Jobs such as engineering, steel making, mending and rebuilding cars, construction. Iron and steel are associated with Mars, as are tools, especially knives.

Medical
Medical emergencies, surgery, surgical instruments.

Competitive Activities
Sports and team games, and especially combat sports such as boxing or wrestling, also competing with colleagues at the place of work and being competitive. Strong man competitions, tournaments, athletics and other major contests.

Agriculture
Mars was one of the gods associated with agriculture, but in this case, it was probably due to the use of iron tools on

the farm, such as ploughs, reapers, scythes and even baling wire.

People in Uniform
Contact with people in the armed services, ambulance service, police, fire service, coastguard, etc.

Warfare
Tradition suggests Mars was a warrior, so this planet rules weapons and warfare, sharp knives, pikes and so forth and guns, explosions and bombs.

Passion and Sex
The other main connection for Mars is passion, male sexuality and sexual energy.

Random Items
Hot temper, road rage, over the top behaviour.

Metal
Iron.

Health
Mars rules red corpuscles, and thus blood, also the head, upper teeth (along with Saturn) accidents, fevers, sudden onset of illness, often something that comes and goes quickly.

Extra Notes

Mars Retrograde
Mars doesn't go retrograde every year, but when it does, it stays in the same area for about seven months. If this happens on your natal Mars, you can expect to be busy during the transit, and you may make decisions that affect

your personal or business life for many years to come. If the retrograde phase makes a sextile or trine aspect to your natal Mars, you can expect a good time, during which you have the energy to fulfil your dreams. If this happens opposite or in square aspect to your natal Mars, you can expect problems and opposition from others and maybe even furious arguments. You may decide to bring a miserable job or an increasingly toxic relationship to an end. Whatever happens, the air will be clearer after the event than it was before the sluggish retrograde phase moved away.

The Signs and Houses

The way that a Mars cycle will play out depends upon whether it is close to an angle or a planet, or which houses are activated by the cycle. For example, a Mars half-return where the natal Mars is in the sixth house and the half-return is coming at it from the twelfth house could bring a health problem or let a skeleton out of the cupboard. Either way, your life could be out of balance for a few days. You need to check out the signs and houses to make sense of these cycles.

Sample Chart

Jimmy Connors
Birth data: 2 September 1952 at 10:30 in East St Louis, USA

Although a Virgoan with a Libra ascendant and an Aquarius Moon, Jimmy's unquenchable Mars is rising in his money-making second house, which is trine to his midheaven, and that helps him succeed.

Jimmy's parents were both into tennis, and he was coached by the best tutors from early childhood, winning his first major competition at the age of twelve. When we look at the next chapter on Jupiter, you will see that twelve is often a good year for wins and successes, but for the

5: Mars

moment, we are considering Mars, which in Jimmy's case, is rising in sporty Sagittarius in his second house.

Jimmy had a great tennis career, and later in life, he coached other winners, which makes sense for someone with Mars in Sagittarius and the Moon in Aquarius, as this would make him a natural coach. He opened a casino on a riverboat at one point. This crazy idea fits with his Sagittarian Mars, Jupiter at the apex of a T-Square and his Aquarius Moon, all of which suggest an interest in unconventional pursuits. This didn't really work out, so he settled for hosting TV game shows (more Saggy influence). Later in life, he had a hip replacement, which is another Mars in Sagittarian theme. Jimmy would be acutely aware of both the Mars and Jupiter transits when they happened because both are powerful influences on his chart.

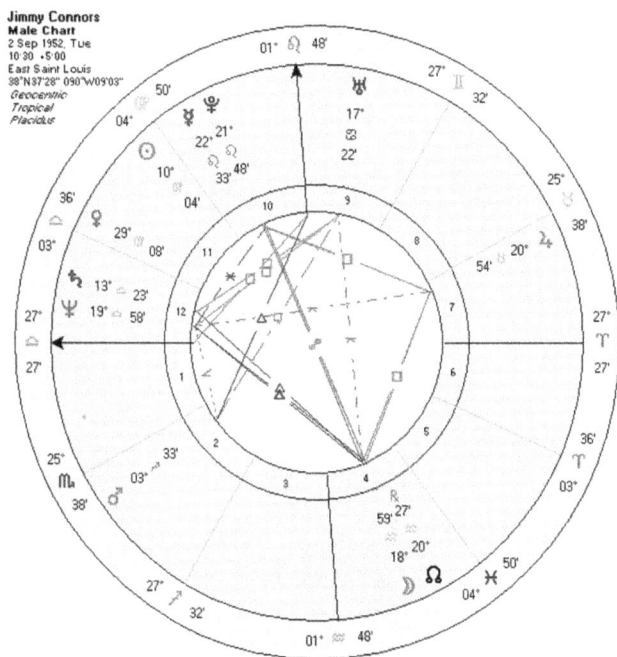

Jimmy Connors - Natal chart

6: Jupiter

JUPITER

Orbit: *42 Earth months. Almost 12 Earth years.*
Symbolic ideas: *The bringer of jollity and a trip beyond boundaries.*

Jupiter is called a transpersonal planet because it is not close to the Earth, but neither is it one of the really distant planets.

The average orbit of Jupiter is just under twelve years, but like all planets, this can vary from one year to the next. In ancient times, astrologers called Jupiter the "great benefic", which has always been associated with luck and opportunity. Jupiter is linked to things that expand our experience of life, so this may shift us out of our comfort zone and take us to new places, teach us new things and bring new people into our lives. Jupiter can kickstart a new love experience, a new work partnership, or new friendships, especially with people from different backgrounds.

Things Associated with Jupiter

Signs of the Zodiac
Sagittarius, and in ancient astrology, also Pisces.

Testing the Limits
The key idea for Jupiter is that of expansion, testing the limits of anything and seeing how far we can go. Jupiter is not into practical matters because it is involved with the worlds of belief, ideas and philosophy. I call Jupiter the "what if" planet because it sends us on journeys of

exploration, which may be physical, intellectual or imaginative.

The Law
The law gives us a framework to work with, such as the Magna Carta or the Declaration of Independence in the USA. The legal system sets the rules for humankind and makes life in a modern democracy safe. It can be used wrongly, of course, but that is also Jupiterian, as this planet is about testing the boundaries.

Belief
The things we believe in or feel about strongly. Also symbolism, which is so important in religions or spiritual thinking.

Religion and Philosophy
Those who become ordained in various religions are often born under the sign of Sagittarius, which is ruled by Jupiter, because it encourages mental exploration of the big questions and the afterlife. Spirituality of all kinds is associated with this planet, as is philosophy and the world of ideas. Jupiter likes to spread the word, so it is associated with evangelism. It is seriously involved with those whose lives are powerfully affected by their own religion or their parents and surrounding society.

Education
Anything that expands the mind comes under Jupiter, but it specifically rules higher or further education.

Foreign Matters
Foreigners, foreign travel, transport over long distances, and business across various countries is ruled by this planet.

Reporting
Jupiter rules journalism, broadcasting and spreading the word in the sense of giving people news, so I guess nowadays, it rules the internet.

Big Animals
Tradition tells us that Jupiter rules horses, and my feeling is that in days before the railways and motor vehicles came into being, using horses to ride or to pull vehicles was the fastest means of travel - apart from sailing ships, that is. Hence the connection with horses, although some people connect Jupiter with all large animals.

Horse Racing
Racing, and by extension, all forms of gambling, are ruled by Jupiter, which could be seen as pushing the boundaries of common sense.

Sports and Games
Jupiter and the Sun rule sports and games, and while Chiron has a claim to fame here, Jupiter would definitely rule an international athletic event.

Metal
Tin.

Health
Jupiter rules the hips, thighs and the liver, so falling and breaking a hip is possible, as are problems with the liver, such as diabetes or cirrhosis, maybe by long-term alcohol abuse or by having to take certain medications over a long time. Jupiter rules expansion, so a major Jupiter aspect can actually expand our waistlines!

6: Jupiter

Jupiter Retrograde

Jupiter goes retrograde when the Sun is in the signs that oppose it. For instance, if Jupiter happens to be in Scorpio at any one time, it will go retrograde while the Sun is in Aries, Taurus and Gemini. Whatever signs it is in, Jupiter retrograde will cause life to slow down for everyone on earth. On a personal note, you will notice things slowing down or even going wrong. It is a bad time to expand a business or call in the builders to enlarge your home. An ordinary holiday will probably be all right, but a long-distance adventure may not work out well. Sports may be a waste of time, and nothing good will come from any form of gambling.

The Signs and Houses

The way that a Jupiter cycle will play out depends upon whether it is close to an angle or a planet, or which houses are activated by the cycle. For example, a Jupiter half-return where the natal Jupiter is in the third house will mess up communications for a while. If the sixth and twelfth houses are involved, there could be a health problem, such as arthritis in the hips or a liver that suddenly becomes sensitive to alcohol or fatty foods. You need to check out the signs and houses to make sense of these cycles.

Now we can really feel the cyclic effects of a planet, because Jupiter makes its return on average around the ages of 12, 24, 36, 48, 60, 72, 84, 96 and 108. As always, it is best to check with an ephemeris or a computer at each of these ages to find the exact date of your own Jupiter returns, but regardless of this, some things seem to work for most people on these return and half-return dates.

The Jupiter squares, sextiles and trines are easy to find by looking up an ephemeris or using astro-software. I have included some interesting stories to bring some of these cycles to life.

Age 6
The Jupiter half-return
Children of this age may struggle at school or with making friends, and as any parent knows, it is a time when children catch childhood illnesses. If the child is growing up in an unhappy household, they will start to notice the misery around them. They need help from their parents, whether for schoolwork, learning to skip or ride a bike, learning to read, or life in general. Some children get the love and help they need, and others don't, so it is worth looking at the natal Jupiter and other factors on a chart while assessing this stage of a child's life.

Age 11 to 12
The Jupiter return
In the UK, children change from a junior school to a higher school at the age of 11; so, after allowing a child time to settle into "big school", children have usually found their feet by the age of twelve, and they make friends, get into sports or gymnastics, enjoy art or drama and having fun in the playground, as well as starting to get a handle on schoolwork. Some youngsters enjoy out-of-school activities, ranging from playing in a band to dancing, skating, sports, art or even just playing with other children. Children may have tests to study for, but they are not yet burdened by cramming for major school exams. The first signs of puberty might be rearing their heads around now for girls, and they may start to take an interest in boys. In general, though, boys start to grow up a bit later.

6: Jupiter

Jane and Me
I was eleven years old, and I hadn't been at the school very long when I became friendly with a girl called Jane, who did the same daily walk back and forth to school like me. One day, I was stuck in the classroom for detention, and when I came out, I expected to find the playground empty, but Jane was waiting for me. I was stupefied. Nobody in my family would have put themselves out to wait for me, but Jane did, and it was evidence of her loyal and generous nature. We have kept in touch, and we still enjoy seeing each other from time to time, and we still chatter and giggle like a pair of kids, much to the amazement of Jane's grandchildren.

Age 18 to 19
The Jupiter half-return
This can be a difficult phase, but it is also the age at which young people start to grow up, and my observation of youngsters over the years makes me think that the brain actually grows and develops more quickly at this time than at any other. Teenagers who have hitherto been totally irresponsible suddenly wake up to the idea of making an effort, and many even come to realise that all the boring guff their parents go on about actually has some value, so they find themselves slowly but surely joining the adult world.

Some youngsters go off to university or attend a technical college now. In contrast, others may join the armed services or some other organisation that brings them into contact with young people from other backgrounds who have different experiences than they do. Jupiter is associated with teaching and studying - especially with further or higher education - and philosophy and belief, so it isn't surprising that this age brings a steep learning curve and an exploration of beliefs. Some young people become political at this time, wanting to improve the world, slow climate change, do something for the disadvantaged, care about animal rights and so on. Some head into a fast and furious round of sexual partnerships, while others experience their first important relationship. Some leave an existing lover behind and find themselves drifting away from them, or maybe it is the lover who drifts away.

Whether youngsters go to university or go straight out to work, the Jupiter effect encourages them to explore relationships with young people from different backgrounds. Some seem to go out of their way to choose their friends and lovers from precisely the type of people who their parents are bound to detest. Here is a story about a young man who went to great lengths to give his parents grief. I have changed his name and identifying information.

Jonathan

Jonathan's parents had worked hard to get out of the working class and into the status and comfort of the middle class. After much sacrifice, Jonathan repaid them well, because he passed his school exams and went to university to study science. It was assumed that in time, Jonathan would choose an upmarket wife, but what he chose appalled his parents. The woman was a waitress several years older than Jonathan, and she was a recent immigrant from some poverty-stricken part of the Far East. While many Asian women are lovely, this girl was far from good looking. The waitress soon set about pushing Jonathan to get a really good job, and she made serious plans about bringing her family over to the UK to enjoy a life they could only dream of in their backward village - naturally, all this at Jonathan's expense.

At some point, it penetrated Jonathan's brain that he was on the brink of marrying another version of his upwardly mobile parents, so he dumped the waitress and eventually married a pretty, English girl from a middle-class family. He never became more than averagely successful, though.

When Jonathan's sister reached her Jupiter return, she turned her back on the parents who had never valued her or liked her, and she emigrated to Australia, where she met a man who was interested in breeding and racing horses. The daughter and her husband became respected, successful and extremely wealthy. Interestingly, Jupiter rules long-distance travel, foreigners, adventure, horses and horse breeding and racing. It clearly worked its magic on both these siblings in different ways.

Age 24 to 25
The Jupiter return
This is usually a happy phase when people are planning their weddings and producing offspring. Whether in marriage, single parentage or extended family groups, this is the time of fertility and young adulthood. It is also an expensive time, but Jupiter is all about expansion, and it is quite happy to lead the young couple into mortgage debt and drain their parents' bank accounts when it comes to weddings and baby expenses. With a bit of luck, the relationships are happy, and parenthood is a pleasure, but even if this isn't the case, this is likely to be the best time of their married or partnered lives. In traditional families, the man makes headway with his career, and the woman makes friends and enjoys motherhood. In less traditional situations, single men and women will be getting ahead and making some kind of home for themselves. These days it is fashionable for young people to spend time at the gym, run half-marathons or get into sports and exercise, but some recognise that they need extra education, all of which is allied to Jupiter.

Age 30
The Jupiter half-return
This coincides with the aftermath of the Saturn return, which marks an important time in everyone's life, so it can be especially effective. Childhood and the youthful twenties are over, so this is when we work out who we are and what we want. This is the time when we are forced to take steps towards meeting our own needs. Some people throw up a deadbeat job and find something that allows them to get ahead; others make serious moves to improve their position at work. Relationships can change at this juncture, with some people getting into a serious partnership for the first time and others deciding to bring a bad relationship to an end. Mothers who have spent much of the last decade at home could return to work, while others start their own businesses, and yet others give up work to have children. It is a time of review and change, often in response to dissatisfaction.

Age 36
The Jupiter return
This is an important time for growth, so career matters or important interests clamour for attention because the person is at their strongest, ablest and most potent. Opportunities can open up, and new jobs and new directions beckon. Some take training courses so they can move up the ladder, and others travel away from home on business.

This is a time of serious change for women, especially in connection with pregnancy. Women who never wanted children can find themselves pregnant and having to decide what to do for the best. Similarly, those who were too busy for children before may find themselves pregnant by accident or by choice. Some of these late-ish pregnancies can be strange, so there are instances of women who only

6: Jupiter

discover they are pregnant when the pregnancy is advanced. There are women whose children have grown and who now decide to put off a return to the world of work by having another baby, while others are horrified to find themselves pregnant just when they thought they could do something interesting in the world of work. Many have miscarriages, while others become sterilised. A surprising number of women find themselves on the way to becoming grandparents now.

Even without the childbirth aspect of this return, women can marry, divorce, change from straight to gay or gay to straight, get good jobs, change careers or disappear into the Amazonian jungle, because the urge to make life worth living becomes overwhelming. Some become widowed and must find their way forward alone.

Age 42
The Jupiter half-return
This follows the Uranus half-return that occurs around the age of 39 to 40. As you will see in the chapter on Uranus, that is always a dramatic event, so this Jupiter opposition can feel like fate is putting yet another nail in the coffin of some aspect of your life. This may work out for the best in the end, but it will be tough to live through for a while. Depending on the position of your natal Jupiter, this could make communications with others difficult, or it could take people who you rely on out of your life, leaving you to cope without them.

Neptune is likely to be square to your natal Neptune at around the age of 41. You may be unsure of your feelings for your current partner, you may have unrealistic feelings for a past partner, for someone else's partner or unrealistic hopes of getting together with a new partner. The half-return could bring an unworkable relationship, or even a "dream relationship" that hasn't turned into reality to a complete ending. This may be painful, but it is probably for the best.

You realise now that you are on the cusp of middle age, with all the unpleasant effects that this brings, such as men getting increasingly bald and putting on weight or feeling more tired than before. Some women will have to face the fact that their chances of giving birth to a healthy child are diminishing, while others will opt for sterilization at this time. Marriages can come or go, and dissatisfaction can set in all around. Those who excelled at sports will find they are slower and less accurate than they once were, and a sports career or a shot at the Olympics is sliding away, leaving the sporting side of life as nothing more than a hobby from now on. Those who were (or thought they were) young and hip enough to be disc jockeys or popular radio presenters may find themselves being by-passed by younger people.

However, the events of this age and stage may not be a total disaster because new doors can open and new roads can appear, and you should probably take them. The worst thing you can do is to try and turn the clock back or hang on to people and situations that have gone.

Age 48
The Jupiter return
We are definitely looking at the start of middle age now, with all the changes this brings. Jupiter is associated with wisdom, so you should know a thing or two about life, love and your work by now. Some of you start businesses of your own, either something on a large and seriously costly scale or small cottage industries that you run from the kitchen table. You are at your most potent by this time, so you will want to forge ahead with your career, perhaps changing from a job that has become stale to one that offers a greater challenge.

6: Jupiter

Your personal life is probably at its best now, but that depends upon your circumstances. Suppose you had children in your teens or early twenties. In that case, they may be in the expensive phase of higher education or may be at work themselves by now. The chances are that they are still at home or at least in contact with you, so the reality of "empty-nest" syndrome hasn't yet struck. Despite the cost of living, your mortgage might be shrinking and your income growing, so life should be at its best at this time. You have enough freedom, time, and money to indulge in hobbies, entertain others, have holidays, and enjoy life. Women may experience the first stirrings of life change with hot flushes, fatigue, night sweats and brain-fug hovering on the horizon.

Age 54
The Jupiter half-return
This does not seem to coincide with any other major planetary event, so it may slide by without causing you too much trouble. I have noticed some people starting to struggle with their jobs at this time, and some may give up formal work in favour of self-employment or freelance jobs. Health matters can rear their head now, while middle age takes hold. Women may be in the throes of the change of life, or they may be through the other side of it and glad to be finished with periods or the danger of pregnancy. South Asian Indian women who had to hide away from the world for years are now out of purdah and can walk around and do more or less what they want with their lives.

Those men and women who loved being parents and who defined themselves by being involved in their children's lives now must adjust to being without their offspring. Work could go well now, but there is likely to be opposition that will push you into making adjustments. Some of you may call in the builders and then live with all the upheaval this brings, or you may move house. It isn't likely to be a bad time, but it can be irritating.

Age 60
The Jupiter return
This follows the Saturn return, so it is a culmination of a period of upheaval, but it should smooth things over and allow for a fresh start. In Chinese astrology, this is the end of the 60-year cycle, which marked the end of life in olden times.

However, now that we are all living so much longer, this could nearly mark the halfway point for many of us! The truth is that this is the start of the third great cycle of life, which is youth, maturity and old age. In cultures that value age, it is considered to be a time of wisdom. Some grandparents who are close to their grandchildren now receive more love and affection than they had from their own children or their partners, and they relish every day of their lives. Others could do without the company of children but enjoy time spent with large or small animals. Some people retire at this age, either because they want to or because that is the policy of their workplace. If they have a good pension and good health, this can be the start of a lovely phase, in which they can enjoy sports, the company of friends or artistic pursuits. For others, health problems start to creep up, curtailing some of the things they were once able to do.

Age 66
The Jupiter half-return
At around this age, I went through a difficult phase that might ring bells with others of the same age. I should have received a pension from the government, but something went wrong, and I had to fight hard to get anywhere.

6: Jupiter

Well, we all have different life experiences, but money problems, pensions that should be paid or that aren't adequate, or work troubles, friends who leave, losses and sadness can strike at this time, as can ill-health. However, the half-return only really holds sway for a few months, so we soon put it behind us and move on.

Age 72
The Jupiter return
This can coincide with an approaching Saturn half-return that may be brewing up trouble behind the scenes, so health problems may build up. Otherwise, this is quite a good time, albeit one of change. Some may now decide to retire, or they may be forced to do so by the people for whom they work. If you are in a good relationship, you should enjoy hobbies, interests, holidays and so on together. Grandchildren should bring pleasure, and life should be pretty good. You may start to take an interest in spiritual matters or perhaps take up astrology at this time.

Age 78
The Jupiter half-return
Like all Jupiter oppositions, this could bring changes that you would rather not have. These could relate to health or life in general. You will likely lose friends now and possibly lose close family members. The main problem here is loneliness, so you must try to join others and be a friend to those in need, as this will bring friendship your way. You also need to do all you can to look after your own health from now on. You can improve your mental health by getting out and about, spending time in the countryside, gardening, flying kites and having fun, joining clubs or groups of like-minded people, helping with some local political group, and doing something other than feeling sorry for yourself or becoming a boring old codger with outdated fixed opinions.

Age 84
The Jupiter return
This is a good time to look back and immortalise your memoirs on a keyboard or paint pictures from your past. Some organisations are happy to employ older people, finding them more reliable, nicer and more capable than those a quarter their age. Obviously, there will be health issues and a lack of strength, and as the Duke of Edinburgh famously said when someone asked him how he was coping with old age, "Bits and pieces drop off, you know".

So, the main thing is to keep going as well as you can. Maybe you can help younger family members by giving them the benefit of your knowledge and experience. For instance, if you are good at do-it-yourself and your grandchildren are attempting it for the first time, grandma or grandpa could come to their rescue to the benefit of all concerned.

This phase coincides with the Uranus return, and it may sweep in on the tail of the Neptune half-return. Hence, it seems that the dreams you once had might never be achievable. Still, there may be spiritual insight and love that you can give to others; also, so many people live up to and more than a hundred years these days, making it imperative that you don't give up the ghost but find things that interest you and keep going.

Age 96
The Jupiter half-return
It is unlikely that you will learn to ride a unicycle now, get a busy job, or take a trip to Hawaii. Indeed, you may spend most of your time sitting about, but the best thing you can do is to keep your mind active, because if you lose that,

you lose everything. Sure, your body is running down, but that's life, and you can cope with that.

Helena's story
My lovely mother-in-law was in a care home where she was happy. A nun had befriended her and visited her regularly, as did Jan and I. She was surrounded by people who were kind to her and who made her comfortable. As a matter of interest, we noticed that her room clock had stopped, and it had got stuck at 6.22 pm. Jan meant to ask for a step ladder so he could change the clock's battery, but before he got round to this, his mum died - and she did so at 6.22 in the afternoon!

Age 102
The Jupiter return
Well, if you're still here and if you're reading this, that's amazing. Good luck to you!

Extra Notes

Signs and Houses
It is always worth checking out the signs and houses involved in a return or half-return to see how it might play out. For instance, a natal Jupiter in Libra would denote a love of justice and a desire for harmony, so a return to that Jupiter would bring injustice to light and make for a more harmonious phase. A half-return might bring hostility or unpleasantness. A Jupiter return to a fourth house natal Jupiter would bring luck to the household. If the fourth house Jupiter were being pressured by a half-return from the tenth house, work, business and even the person's reputation would be under attack.

Quarter-return (square) transits to natal Jupiter coming from the seventh house might set off marriage

Astrological Cycles In Focus

problems and so on. A point to consider is the signs involved, because Jupiter in adventurous Aries or Sagittarius is different from Jupiter in emotional Scorpio or cautious Virgo.

The Jupiter Factor
Many sportspeople have Jupiter in an angular house, especially the seventh or tenth houses. Here are a few.

1st House Jupiter	Jackie Chan
4th House Jupiter	Jack Nicklaus
7th House Jupiter	Bjorn Borg
7th House Jupiter	Billie Jean King
10th House Jupiter	Alan Shearer
10th House Jupiter	Mohammed Ali

7: Saturn

SATURN

Orbit: *29.5 Earth years.*
Symbolic ideas: *Limitation, reality, career success, authority, the bringer of old age.*

Saturn is called a transpersonal planet because it is not close to the Earth, but neither is it so far away that it can't be seen with the naked eye.

The orbit of Saturn means we experience the first return at around 29.5 years, but the changes can be felt well before it reaches the exact aspect. This is even more the case with the second Saturn return, which should take place at the age of 58, but which often kicks in a year or two earlier.

When people start to learn astrology, the Saturn returns are the first cycles they discover, and they soon learn how effective these are. When new students discover how limiting Saturn can be, they swiftly decide they dislike Saturn, but without Saturn, nothing would get done. You could call Jupiter the "what if" planet because it is associated with belief, ideas and philosophy, and has nothing to do with practical matters. Saturn is the opposite, as it is all about practicality, and without it, nothing would exist. Here are a few things with which Saturn is associated.

Things Associated with Saturn

Signs of the Zodiac
Capricorn, and in ancient astrology, also Aquarius.

7: Saturn

Practical Matters
Saturn rules all that is sensible, down to earth and useful in our daily lives. It sets boundaries, gives us rules to live by and is associated with the hard work that needs to go into anything before it can come to fruition. A tree has roots that ensure it receives nutrition and that keep it from falling down, and a house needs foundations, but it also needs tangible items such as furniture, appliances and floor coverings. We all need to learn how to do things before we become experts, and studying can be tedious at times, so when we consider maths, architecture and even our everyday struggles with computer software, we see how Saturn invades every part of our lives. We get home feeling tired from a day's work, but we still must make a meal, do the chores and clear the decks before we can sink into oblivion on the sofa. All this is typical of Saturn.

Time and Chronology
Saturn rules the passing of time, clocks, watches and probably even egg timers! It rules things that take time, but it also tells us the right time to do something, especially if it requires effort. It rules specialized machinery such as instruments, weights, measures and calculations, and it definitely rules computers and office machinery!

Karma
Saturn is the lord of karma, so what goes around comes around when Saturn is active.

Discipline and Self-Discipline
Saturn rules endurance, persistence, caution and restraint, not making a fuss, getting down to things, making an effort, organisation and self-motivation.

Father Figures and Authority Figures
Some astrologers view Saturn on a natal chart as the person's father, but whether that is the case or not, Saturn represents authority figures, whether they are male, female, related to us or not. Saturn represents the leader whose rules we are obliged to obey at work or any other sphere of life.

Status
This is the person with the big reputation, the big boss and the one we admire. It links with leadership, arrogance, and often with pride going before a fall.

Ambition and Achievement
This is the motivating factor for many of us, so whatever ambition we have, Saturn helps us achieve it.

Maturity
This planet is associated with senior citizenship, old age and wisdom.

Suffering
Some aspects of pain and suffering are involved here, especially chronic health problems or ongoing life situations, such as looking after a disabled child or an older family member with Alzheimer's disease. It rules aggravation and limitation.

Politics
Saturn rules national politics and politicians, power and authority.

Big Organisations
This can be banks, building societies, insurance companies, political parties, big business, corporate matters.

7: Saturn

Religion
In times gone by, Saturn ruled religion and even astrology, and it still rules the organisational aspects of religion.

Agriculture
Saturn was a god that ruled agriculture, and even the ancient symbol of the man holding a reaper demonstrates that something has been grown and is now being cut down.

Construction and Similar.
Saturn also rules masonry, building tools, trees, furniture and coffin makers. As a writer, I would ascribe books to Saturn and articles to Mercury or Jupiter.

Metal
Lead

Health
Saturn rules the bones, skin and hearing. It is associated with old age, so it rules hardening of the arteries, arthritis, ageing and a general slowing down of the mind and body.

Random Ideas
Saturn was said to be dour, overly religious, pessimistic and dull, but people who have a strong Saturn are often cheerful, chatty, humorous, good company, helpful and kind, family loving and even slightly sporty, so the old ideas about Saturn just don't hold water.

Age 7 to 8
The Saturn Quarter Return
I am not going to go through all the quarter-returns, but this is worth mentioning because it hits many children badly and is a point where something really nasty can happen. It doesn't cause every child a problem, but the instances of things going badly wrong at this age are legion. The worst-case scenario is the death of a parent or one that walks out and is never heard from again. The child may get ill, or a parent may be very ill at this time, or something else may happen that is seriously traumatic. One really bad experience is of some family member, a step relative, or a family friend starting a regime of abuse.

Robert was eight years old when his father had bypass surgery, and that frightening period is something he has never forgotten.

Age 14 to 15
The Saturn Half-Return
This is when the hormones are running at full pelt, so love, sex and desire enter the picture, and many youngsters fall deeply in love at this time. It may be called puppy love, but the feelings can be overwhelming and unforgettable. Unrequited love rarely works out well and it is rarely pleasant or successful.

This is when childhood starts to slip away, and some aspects of this are welcome, while others are not. For instance, the young person has more freedom than before, but school becomes more serious with exams looming and having to decide whether to take further education, an apprenticeship or avoid making any kind of effort at all.

7: Saturn

Age 29
The Saturn Return
This is the famous first Saturn return, and it is something that affects every one of us. I have known people who have done extremely well at this time because they used their Saturn positively to push ahead with a career, and such people earn good money and spend it on sensible Saturnian things such as property or premises. Some settle into marriage-type relationships, have children and start to take life seriously, while others realise they are with the wrong person and wake up to the fact that sooner or later, they are likely to leave their partners. It is the time when carefree youth has to be set aside for the serious side of adulthood, and it plays out in many ways. Some women who had children when they were young go back to work, while others change their careers. Whatever the case may be, there is always a dose of reality at this time.

While writing this, I have just asked a friend of ours called Peter if anything important happened when he was 29, and he said that his eldest daughter was born then.

Obviously, becoming a parent means taking on responsibility, but it also shows two other things. Firstly, the Saturn return is often felt before it arrives - in this case, during the months of pregnancy that precede the arrival of the little one. Secondly, it also proves that not everything Saturn brings is bad, but it does bring obligations and accountability. Saturn makes us face facts.

Apparently, the U.S. census reports a peak of divorces around age 30 when promises made in youth turn to dust. Sometimes Saturn may bring a karmic relationship that may be intense and passionate, but the usual rule is that of commitment. Some people get downhearted at this age and must face the fact that something is not working, so if it isn't the relationship that is hitting the rocks, it might be realising that we've chosen the wrong career path. Perhaps we need to call time on an impossible relationship with difficult parents or step-relatives or move away from hellish neighbours. If you have been drifting along for years, you will realise that you must get down to things now, so it is time to find out what matters, make something of yourself, and work towards your goals.

Age 44
The Saturn Half-Return
Oddly enough, for such an important planet as Saturn, the half-return in the mid-forties doesn't have the same reputation as the Saturn return, and one possibility is that it doesn't always seem to cause a problem. This is the age at which we should have a good career and a settled and happy family life, but for some people, this is not the case. The first signs of aging start to show themselves, perhaps by discovering that we need glasses for reading or using a computer. We may give up smoking or cut back on drinking, and we may be less inclined to spend our nights clubbing than to spend it dozing in an armchair. It is all starting to catch up with us. Saturn can hit some people badly on this half-return, and I have known those who become bereaved due to losing a parent or a partner on this opposition.

Age 56 - 58
The Saturn Return
This is another important return, and the "biggies" are health, relationships and work. We get tired, and we are not as flexible as we were. Menopause can be hard on women. Builders no longer whistle at us when we sashay past them

7: Saturn

in the street, and we realise with sadness that we have become invisible.

Many men and women become grandparents at this time, and that makes some people feel very old. In some cases, the women take on caring for their grandchildren, which is yet another aspect of Saturnian burdens. Our parents and in-laws may need more help from us just when the children are costing us a fortune at university or needing help to buy their first homes. Some suffer from "empty nest syndrome" when the children leave home to go their own way. If our marriages and family life are good, that is great. Still, for those who have struggled for years with a rotten relationship, the fact that the children are no longer dependent upon them may encourage them to leave the marriage.

Jobs and careers should be going well as we reach the higher echelons of the workplace, and we should now have self-respect and the respect of others. Some may change at this stage, looking for a better job or even something completely different. Some have the time and inclination to develop an interest in spirituality at this time. A lovely friend of mine called Gordon Arthur Smith had a heart attack on this return and had to retire from his job as an engineer. Fortunately, he could earn money by giving psychic readings, so he got by until he died on his next Saturn half-return at the age of 72.

Rachel's Story
Rachel had a friend called Amelia who had it all - including a loving husband who worked in the kind of job where he was "on-call" much of the time, rather than actually working. So, he spent his days helping Amelia care for their three pretty little girls while also extending and improving their small house. Amelia's parents spent much of their time helping her as well, so Amelia was able to spend her days

taking her little car to the shops to buy stuff for the house and lots of pretty clothes for herself. After a while, Amelia and her family moved away, and Rachel didn't see her again for many years; then, Rachel bumped into her one day.

She hardly recognised the exhausted, old-looking woman. It transpired that the husband had developed a disability and no longer worked, the father had died, the girls had grown up, moved away, and frankly, didn't want to know Amelia. Her mother was now a demanding old lady who lived close by. Amelia had a demanding job, and she was clearly worn out. The poor girl was on her second Saturn return, and it was hitting her with a vengeance. Rachel was sorry for her, but it proved to Rachel that nobody escapes the Lord of Karma.

Lisa's Story
Like many of us, Lisa has been married and divorced and had brought up her children to the point where they had left home to pursue their own dreams. She now met a lovely man who she fell in love with and married. He came from a different country, and the happy couple went to live there. This was all fine, but it brought unexpected responsibilities and things that required effort, such as learning a new language, getting used to a new set of relatives and living in a very different environment. Saturn always requires effort and some form of extra responsibility.

Approximate Age 72
The Saturn Half-Return
I say approximate age now, because as time goes by, the returns and half-returns may occur sooner than they should, but somehow 72 does seem to be an age at which changes happen to us, partly because this is also a Jupiter return. Obviously now, we are looking at senior citizenship, so health is the biggest issue, and there is bound to be

7: Saturn

something that we must handle. Another common experience for many subjects at this age is losing good friends and loved relatives to death. A friend of mine lost 23 people in the same year, which happened to be the year of her Saturn half-return.

Relationships come and go, and possibly, those who had enough of being mistreated may call it a day on this opposition, but some people meet new lovers at this point as well. The problem is that Saturn doesn't give us an easy ride, so new lovers might choose to be with us because they are worried about their own health and want someone to look after them, or perhaps they have recently come out of a difficult relationship and need someone to put a roof over their heads and pay their way. It really is a case of weighing it all up and seeing what is important, because taking on someone in dire straits might prove to be better than continuing to be alone.

Some people are still working at this stage, but the likelihood is that they are self-employed or freelance. Whether they work because they enjoy what they are doing or because they need the money depends on their circumstances. Others are delighted to be free of work and happy to spend time on hobbies and interests that they enjoy.

Approximately Age 95 to 100
Saturn Return
Once again, this is an approximate time scale, as the effects can come sooner. This is when others appreciate our wisdom and experience, and we come to terms with whatever spiritual beliefs we have. We can still love others, but the desires and lusts of youth have gone, and ambition is a thing of the past. Some people become national treasures, such as "Captain" Tom Moore, the Duke of Edinburgh and of course, Queen Elizabeth, who is still doing a full day's work in her nineties. Some enjoy their

Astrological Cycles In Focus

pets, gardens or hobbies at this age, but sadly others lose their health or faculties and are getting ready to pass over.

Extra Notes

The Saturn Factor
Here are a few people who have an angular Saturn, and in many cases, you can see how it pushed them to work hard, overcome problems, and achieve their ambitions.

Saturn in 1st house - Margaret Thatcher
A hard-working Prime Minister who famously made do with very few hours of sleep.

Saturn in 1st house - Russell Grant
A hard-working astrologer and writer with Meniere's disease affecting the ears, and as he knows very well, Saturn rules the ears and hearing.

Saturn as the rising planet on the cusp of the 1st and 2nd houses - Mark Spitz
Olympic gold medal swimmer.

Saturn in 4th house - Cary Grant
After a childhood from hell, Cary worked hard and became an international film star.

Saturn on the 7th house cusp - David Cameron
A Prime Minister whose eldest child was very handicapped and who died young.

Saturn in the 10th house - Lech Walesa
Very brave Polish Prime Minister who took Poland out of the Soviet bloc and out of communism.

7: Saturn

Saturn in the 10th house - Jeffrey Archer
This man has had his ups and downs, but he's still working now that he has recovered from cancer. Astrological tradition says that Saturn in the tenth house brings fame and fortune and public disgrace, and both have been the case for Jeffrey.

8: Uranus

URANUS

Orbit: *84 Earth years.*
Symbolic ideas: *Originality, unpredictability, change, progress.*

Uranus is called an impersonal planet because it is a long way from the Earth, and it cannot be seen with the naked eye. The orbit of Uranus means that not everyone lives long enough to experience the Uranus return. At the same time, the half-return often kicks in a couple of years before its due date, which could be because the run-up to the exact transit is often as effective as the transit itself. If we keep to the rules, the return should arrive at the age of 84, the half-return or opposition should occur at the age of 42 and the quarter-return or square at the age of 21 and a second quarter-return or square at the age of 63, but the effect of Uranus is often felt before the exact transit.

Things Associated with Uranus

Sign of the Zodiac
Aquarius

Upheavals
An astrologer friend of mine once described Uranus as the "breakout planet" because it forces us to break out of routines and change our lives in one way or another. My feeling is that this is the most fateful planet of the solar system, because things can happen out of the blue that seem like fate or destiny. It is associated with upheaval, revolution, changes in habits, lifestyles and changes. It is

associated with technology, new ideas and unconventional ways of doing things, but as far as our lives are concerned, Uranus can set off a range of effects, such as sudden job and relationship changes and much more. Without this planet, nobody would invent anything, and we'd still be getting around by horse and cart and lighting our homes by candlelight!

Politics and Movements
Groups who come together to achieve something could involve political activities, especially green, humanitarian or idealistic ones. Any new movements, especially those that help humanity, animals, the climate or anything else on a somewhat impersonal scale. Uranus rules causes and soapboxes but also local politics, while Saturn rules national politics.

Group Activities
On a smaller scale than above, Uranus rules group activities, clubs, committees, societies and anything that brings like-minded people together. A fun run that raises money for a cause would be typical, as would working on the local council or joining the committee of *The Federation of Small Businesses*, *The Astrological Association* or a million other special interest groups.

Friends and Acquaintances
Uranus rules detached relationships, such as friendships, groups of friends and acquaintances rather than very close relationships.

Ideas and Education
Concepts, new ideas, new beliefs, inventions and anything new or out of the ordinary. Uranus is also associated with teaching and learning, schools, colleges and universities.

Technology
Uranus rules technology, and the massive increase in the speed of invention indicates that we are now in the age of Aquarius.

Attitudes
This planet is linked to unconventionality, eccentricity, individualism, independence, self-motivation, stubbornness and determination.

Events
Uranus rules shocks, surprises, upheavals, changes in attitude, and life changes.

Metal
Uranium.

Health
Uranus is associated with ankles, calves and Achilles' tendon. Also, accidents and sudden onsets of an ailment, physical, mental and emotional shocks.

Age 20 to 21
The Uranus Quarter-Return
This is a time of growth, so where work is concerned, this is when we start to put our minds to things. A relative of mine left school at sixteen with no qualifications and drifted in and out of a variety of dead-end jobs, but at the age of twenty, he decided to train as become a London taxi driver. The course is rigorous and takes two years to complete, but his decision led to a career that lasted the rest of his working life, giving him a good income and lots of friends, which suited him very well because he is a friendly guy. I have also known women who had good careers but who threw

them up at this age in favour of marriage and children. So, as you can see, changes can come from one direction or another, from our own internal psyche or outside influence. These changes can be positive or negative, but they make us think about what we want.

Students may drop out or be happy to have completed their course and look forward to finding a good job and getting on with their adult lives. Needless to say, this is an age when many choose a partner and start their own families, while some realise they have made a mistake and even go through the trauma of terminating a pregnancy. Anything can happen, and it usually does.

Age 39 to 42
The Uranus Half-Return
This is a big event that will affect everyone on earth in some way or another. It can affect any aspect of life, but one typical change comes when we realise that a bad relationship needs to end. However, this can also be a time when we meet someone new. Some people realise they are gay at this time and decide against continuing to live an inauthentic lifestyle. Job and career changes are also possible because people get tired of what they have done for so long and feel urged to look for something new. Some stay in an adequate marriage and job but take up exciting new interests and hobbies or learn something new. Some become sporty; others become spiritual, and so on. Here are two stories of the kind of sudden changes that can happen at this age.

Melvin's Story
Melvin's relationship had ended in a burst of unpleasantness on both sides, but now Melvin met a new woman online. The new lady was also going through a nasty divorce, but she moved in with Melvin, and in no time

at all, the happy couple were married, proving that Uranus isn't one for hanging about. Melvin was convinced he'd found his soul mate, but the woman turned out to be a hopeless alcoholic, so a few years later, Melvin off-loaded her in yet another costly divorce. He says he won't rush into any more marriages in future - whatever Uranus is doing on his chart!

Susan's Story
Susan was in a long-standing relationship with a married man who was becoming increasingly possessive and abusive, criticising her work, her behaviour, and even her religion and ethnicity. He constantly accused her of sleeping with every man she met, including her own brother. Susan realised that the situation was making her miserable, and it was outweighing her love for the man, so when the Uranus half-return came around, she left him. Enough was enough.

Age Around 63
The Uranus Quarter-Return
This transit can be difficult, and it can somehow become bound up with professional people and authority figures, which is an odd situation because that is normally the realm of Saturn. Some of the effects that I have come across are people who fall ill and join the struggle of trying to get help from the National Health Service, or those who try hard to get a proper pension out of a company they have worked for or out of the government's Pension Service. Others are desperate to stay at work, but their bosses want to get rid of them.

Marriages that have struggled for years can suddenly come to an end, and people can even start new relationships at this age. People who find themselves alone or with someone more easy-going than their former partner

8: Uranus

may acquire a pet that they can enjoy at this time. Some discover spirituality, while others take up art or grow flowers in window boxes. In short, this transit can bring an important change or a fairly minor one, but with Uranus being the unpredictable planet that it is, one can't say for certain what the change will be.

This can be the start of old age, and while some people sink into decrepitude at this time, others get a new lease of life and find something new to do with themselves. I have known people taking up ballroom dancing and getting a great social life as a result, but I have also known others who died on this transit.

Age Around 84

The Uranus Return
This coincides with a Jupiter return, and it can include other planetary returns and half-returns, so it is an important age. Would someone consider starting a new business at this time? Well, yes, actually, because that's just what my mother did, and it kept her happy for the next few years. I knew one woman who had always been in very good health, but as the Uranus return struck, she was involved in a bad road accident and had to have one of her legs rebuilt; she was never out of pain after that date. So, such things as arthritis, bad eyesight and hearing, or dreaded dementia might strike at around this age, but so can spirituality or the desire to write a book or two. We have helped several people of this age group self-publish memoirs, histories of their area and novels, all of which has given them a great deal of pleasure at this late stage of their lives.

Age Around 106
The Uranus Quarter-Return
Well, people are living this long, and this must be a time of reckoning when their health or their lives are coming to an end. Let's hope they look back with happiness and put the famous message on their gravestone that Lady Caroline Lamb did, which said: "It's all been very interesting..."

Extra Notes
Interestingly, many recent politicians have Uranus in the twelfth house, suggesting they use friends and groups to help them work on their strategies behind the scenes. The following all have Uranus in angular houses.

Uranus in the 1st house - Charles de Gaulle
A famous French President who helped the French to regain their dignity after World War Two. He didn't like the British, though, and he didn't hide his feelings about the UK.

Uranus in the 1st house - Oliver Cromwell
Some like Oliver Cromwell and some don't, but nobody can deny that he was an important historical personage. He had Charles I executed and became the Lord Protector of England and Wales for eleven years, until his death from natural causes.

Uranus in the 1st house - Anthony Armstrong Jones
This man was noted for being married to Princess Margaret, which couldn't have been easy. He was also artistic, a good photographer and designer. He was bi-sexual and highly sexed.

8: Uranus

Uranus in the 1st house - Audrey Hepburn
Lovely Belgian film star, who barely survived starvation in Holland in the latter stages of World War Two and then became a major film star.

Uranus in the 4th house - Marlene Dietrich
Charismatic international film star and singer with a strange voice. Came across as bi-sexual, but who knows?

Uranus in the 4th house - Antoine de Saint Exupery
A writer whose books seemed on the face of it to be for children, but the stories were too sad for young people.

Uranus in the 7th house - Gerald Depardieu
International film actor, not good looking but charismatic.

Uranus in the 7th house - Paul Theroux
Interesting, slightly satirical writer.

Uranus in the 10th house - Alfred Assolant
A 19th-century author who was one of the early writers of children's books.

Uranus in the 10th house - Heinrich Himmler
The odious Nazi who orchestrated the Holocaust, among other despicable things. About the only thing he had to offer anyone was death.

9: Neptune

NEPTUNE

Orbit: *165 Earth years.*
Symbolic ideas: *Dreams, illusion, escapism, artistry, spirituality, the sea.*

Neptune is an impersonal planet. Its orbit is so long that nobody can live to see the return, and not everyone will live to experience even the half-return, so we will look at the Neptune quarter-returns and maybe one or two one-eighth returns instead. Roughly speaking, the half-return occurs at around the age of 82, so the quarter-return will be at around 41, and a one-eighth transit would occur at around 20 and again at 61. There can be another Neptune eighth return at around 100 plus years.

Things Associated with Neptune

Sign of the Zodiac
Pisces.

Confusion
Neptune was the Roman god of the sea, and our astrological Neptune is also associated with the sea, but it has other associations that are more suited to Morpheus, the god of sleep. However, two of Neptune's moons are Oberon and Titania, and these are the god and goddess of dreams, so the whole thing is something of a muddle, which is typical of Neptune! Neptune represents the highest we can aspire to and the lowest we can sink to, but wherever Neptune gets involved in a person's chart, a certain amount of confusion reigns.

9: Neptune

The Higher Realms
Neptune is not interested in the basic requirements of food, clothing and shelter because it is attuned to higher matters, and it is linked to the things we hope for in our dreams. If you are into the chakra system, you can consider Neptune to be associated with the higher chakras, such as the brow and crown chakra.

Revelations
Things that have been hidden or growing quietly behind the scenes can suddenly reveal themselves. Sometimes the person suspects there is something wrong but can't get anyone to listen. This may be a betrayal in a relationship or some health problem that eventually comes to light.

Falling in Love
When we fall in love, we are at our happiest and most excited by life. We can't even go down with a cold or feel ill because our hearts, minds and bodies are too busy being happy. Is this real? Does it last? Well... Neptune isn't about reality; it is about the illusion of reality.

Muddles, Mistakes, Fraud and Betrayal in Business
Mercury is the god of thieves, but Neptune can also do its share of damage. Nothing is quite what it appears to be when Neptune is active, so business and financial arrangements can be difficult and dangerous.

Sacrifice
This planet rules sacrifice on behalf of others, and caring for those who need help.

Misunderstandings and Betrayal in Personal Life
Love affairs and relationships that go wrong are the engines of women's fiction. Still, in real life, a Neptune aspect can be truly devastating, as shown by the classic story of Prince Charles and Princess Diana. If Prince Charles had ignored his weird, unhelpful, interfering and critical family and insisted on marrying Camilla Shand when they were young, despite her not being considered "noble" enough according to his uncle, Louis Mountbatten, it would have worked out well for the two of them. It is amazing that Camilla's lack of nobility no longer matters these days, but what a lot of muddle and unhappiness all this caused everyone concerned over the years.

Film, Recordings, Television
The moment something is recorded, the act of creation has already passed, but the recording can go on forever. I happened to watch the film "Casablanca" on the television the other day; just about everyone who was in it is now dead, but the film lives on, as powerful and fascinating as ever. So, film, television programmes and records or music downloads are not the current reality, but something that no longer exists.

The Arts
All the arts come under the aegis of Neptune, so this includes music, painting, dress design, dance, sculpture, making stained glass or anything else you can imagine. Indeed, imagination itself comes under the rulership of Neptune because it can turn into something real, although imagination doesn't actually exist in its own right. Confused? Well, that's Neptune for you.

9: Neptune

Spirituality

This subject covers everything from established religion, beliefs such as Wicca, spiritualism, and energy healing. Anything that people find uplifting, helpful, beneficial to physical and mental health, or that aids spiritual and psychic development, comes under the rulership of Neptune, as does mediumship, and even some forms of psychotherapy, such as bereavement counselling. It helps those who want to connect with a god or deity, but it also links with the spiritual side of art, music and dancing. These subjects can't be accessed by the five senses but are linked to the sixth sense that can only be understood by those who develop it.

Escapism

Many forms of escape from the stresses of normal life are well worth doing. The person who finds it relaxing to make a cake, weed the garden, fly a kite, watch a soap on the television, or play with a train set in the loft is escaping real life for a while, and that is a healthy thing to do. However, using alcohol or drugs is a road to destruction. In time, it destroys the users themselves, their partnerships, their wider families and everything they touch. Yet, the desire to become a zombie is so powerful that children as young as ten or eleven make a start on this road despite the well-known dangers. Millions of adults still choose this option in preference to living authentically.

Hospitals, Prisons, Asylums and Places of Seclusion

Neptune rules places of seclusion, whether someone decides to spend most of their life away from people or whether they are sent away against their will for some reason. I have noticed that those with a strong Neptune at birth or who are born under the sign of Pisces often spend some time in hospital or confined to their bed during childhood.

The Sea and Water
There is a practical side to Neptune, and it is the link to the sea and water in general, so it concerns everyone who lives and works on the sea or near water. It includes swimming pools, water parks, lidos, lakes, rivers, fish and fishing. Tides, waves, tsunamis, storms at sea and those that cause flooding on land, heavy rain and danger at sea or in water show that this planet is not as soft as it looks.

Animals
This planet can be linked to a fondness for animals, and planetary cycles can bring a pet or two into someone's life.

Metal
I don't think there is a metal associated with Neptune, but how about a meteorite?

Health
Neptune is linked to health in general, especially chronic ailments such as asthma, auto-immune ailments and even the Covid19 virus and others of the kind. Tradition links Neptune with the feet, but the lungs, body fluids, and lymphatic system also fall under Neptune's rulership.

Approximate Age 20 to 21
The Neptune Eighth Return

This makes Neptune sextile to its natal position. It's quite common for people to meet the one they want to spend their lives with at this age, so this transit is associated with love and partnerships. Not every relationship is worth having, though, as there can be hidden agendas

9: Neptune

and hidden problems. Another frequent event at this age – particularly for women - is falling pregnant.
Many youngsters finish their education at this time and look for their dream job. Whether they find it or not is an interesting point.

Approximate Age 41 to 42
The Neptune Quarter-Return
This is when Neptune is square to its natal position, and being a slow-moving outer planet, it takes time for the problem to show itself. Neptune can set off any number of events, some of which take us by surprise. This planet is linked to mental and physical health, so the person might go down with some hard-to-diagnose ailment or go through a period of loss and unhappiness. Neptune being such a weird planet, the reasons for any of these things can be obscure.

Approximate Age 62 to 63
The Neptune Eighth Return
This can be a surprisingly eventful time that brings some real problems. It is not unusual for a long marriage to come to an end at this time, possibly because one or both partners retire from work and must decide whether they want to spend their days with their spouse or not. Others might decide that they have done all they can for their partner, children, grandchildren and so on and can't face being with the same partner or in the same family group any longer. Some go out shopping and never come back.
    Illness can strike, and even those who have been well all their lives can become ill. The feet seem to be particularly vulnerable, so accidents and incidents involving the feet might occur now.

Astrological Cycles In Focus

Approximate Age 82 to 83
Neptune Half-Return
This is the start of a very active phase on everyone's chart, when many planets make important aspects that can have a powerful effect on a person's life, and it can take a few years before the effect of all this becomes known. Neptune is associated with health, so this is often when a fall, a road accident or an illness befalls the subject and brings major problems, especially relating to the legs, feet or lungs. It is not an easy time.

As it happens, I came across something interesting article in the newspaper, in which a man of 82 had been trying to work out why he was paying a monthly sum for an iPad that he bought years ago, which had long since come to the end of its life. The newspaper correspondent took this up with the company from which the man had bought the tablet and discovered that the poor man had been sold a totally unnecessary insurance policy for the product, which brought in extra money for the company, but which they had no obligation to warn him about, and even less obligation to tell him to stop paying after a reasonable time. After the correspondent got on to them, the company repaid a very small amount of this money and kept the rest for themselves. Neptune is all about muddles and scams, so this is an example of just such an incident.

9: Neptune

Approximate Age 102 to 103
Neptune Eighth Return
It would be tempting to think nothing can happen at this age, but it can. The Queen Mother and Captain Tom died at this age. Neptune is a very spiritual planet, so perhaps this is signalling a time when our return to "the other side" is drawing near.

Extra Notes
It might be worth checking the charts of famous musicians, artists, spiritual mediums and so on to see if they have a prominent or interesting natal Neptune. Here are a couple that might kickstart your research.

Taylor Swift
Neptune in Capricorn in the second house shows she earns her living from her creativity.

Dolly Parton
Neptune in Libra in the second house shows she earns her living from her creativity.

Britney Spears
Neptune in Sagittarius in the third house shows that she doesn't always hear the truth from those around her.

Lady Gaga
Neptune in Capricorn in the seventh house shows her combination of business sense and musicality.

10: Pluto

PLUTO

Orbit: *240 Earth years.*
Symbolic ideas: *Transformation, birth, death, major change.*

Here are some important facts about Pluto:

- Pluto is a dwarf planet that is sometimes inside the orbit of Neptune and sometimes outside of it.
- Pluto's orbit reaches higher and falls lower than other planets, which makes its orbit extremely eccentric.
- Pluto takes 240 years to orbit the Sun.
- When Pluto is at perihelion (nearest to the Sun), it can take as little as thirteen years to traverse a sign, and when at aphelion (furthest from the Sun), it can take as long as thirty-three years to do so.
- Pluto has a large moon called Charon and several smaller moons.
- Pluto's influence is generational as much as personal.

All the above tells us that it is impossible to give a set list of the ages at which Pluto will affect our lives. Having said that, those born around the middle of the 20th century experienced a Pluto quarter-return (Pluto-square-Pluto) around their early to mid-forties. In contrast, those born later will experience it later, and the half-return may or may not come up during a person's lifetime.

Pluto is small and distant, but its effect is mega-powerful, so it is always worth considering Pluto's transits to other planets on your chart, even if you can't make a connection with a Pluto transit to your natal Pluto. Pluto

10: Pluto

transforms everything that it touches, and sometimes it can be hard to live with its effects.

Things Associated With Pluto

Birth, Death and the Passage to the "Other Side"
Each of these concepts involves transformation, which is very Plutonic.

Sarah's Story
Sarah is a lovely lady with the Sun in Scorpio who lived through a bad time when Pluto transited her Sun, retrograded back over the Sun and then crossed it again going forward. This took a couple of years, during which time Sarah's drug-addicted daughter caused much pain and suffering to Sarah until the girl died on the third transit.

Transformation, Recycling, Changing from One State to Another
Even the recycling we do with our bottles and packaging is related to Pluto, as is refurbishing old furniture or making new clothes out of old.

Sex
Sometimes an appearance of sex can be attributed to Pluto even when it may or may not be the case, such as when a sexy-looking film star projects a Plutonic image. The first and second houses are concerned with appearances and image, so Pluto would definitely look sexy here.

Procreation, Committed Relationships
Pluto is particularly associated with shared resources, so relationships and partnerships are part of this, as is sex in connection with procreation. My feeling is that fertility clinics and fertility treatment would come under the rulership of Pluto.

Wills, Legacies, Taxes
Serious legal and financial matters belong to Pluto, as do business and corporate matters, buying and selling stocks and shares, and insurance.

Mining, Excavation, Oil Exploration, Archaeology
Pluto rules the underworld, thus everything that is under the ground.

Butchery, Surgery, Medical Matters
Mercury and Neptune are also associated with health and medicine, but Pluto is linked to the more serious aspects.

Psychiatry
Getting inside someone's head is linked to Pluto.

Forensic Science, Espionage, Counterespionage, Investigation
All these exciting ideas that we love to read about belong to the realm of Pluto. It all comes down to secrets and mysteries and things that are hidden from sight.

Engineering, Military Matters
Mars also rules these items, but Pluto has a hand in them as well.

Power, Behind the Scenes, Secrets and Hidden Things
Anything that is hidden and needs to be winkled out belongs to Pluto, but also to Neptune.

Metal
Not really a metal, but a manufactured element, which is, of course, Plutonium.

10: Pluto

Health
The reproductive organs, lower part of the body, lower part of the spine, and the duodenum. People with a strong Pluto on their chart can't take hot or spicy food as it upsets their digestion.

Extra Notes

I have picked out a few film stars who have a sexy image, so let us see what their Pluto is telling us.

Bridget Bardot
Unsurprisingly, her Pluto is in her eighth house, which relates to Scorpio, which, in turn, is ruled by Pluto.

Michael Caine
Is Michael Caine sexy? He has Pluto in the second house, and it is his rising planet. Interestingly, Michael didn't allow fame and money to go to his head and he has used his wealth wisely, which makes sense with Pluto in this house.

Joan Collins
Joan has her Pluto in the second house, and it is her rising planet. She is definitely sexy, and she has used her money wisely.

Jack Nicholson
Jack is a sexy man, but his Pluto is in the secretive twelfth house, although it is close to his ascendant.

Lawrence Olivier
As a very Geminian personality, Lawrence could be anything he wanted to be, but he had a sexy Pluto rising in the first house.

Astrological Cycles In Focus

Cary Grant
Very fanciable but apparently needy, babyish and possibly bisexual. His Pluto was in the eighth house, but his reality didn't live up to his image.

Dirk Bogarde
Lovely, attractive and gay, Dirk's Pluto was in the first house, and it was his rising planet.

***

Just for fun, here is Brigitte Bardot's natal chart. She was born on September 28th, 1934, at 13:15 in Paris, France.

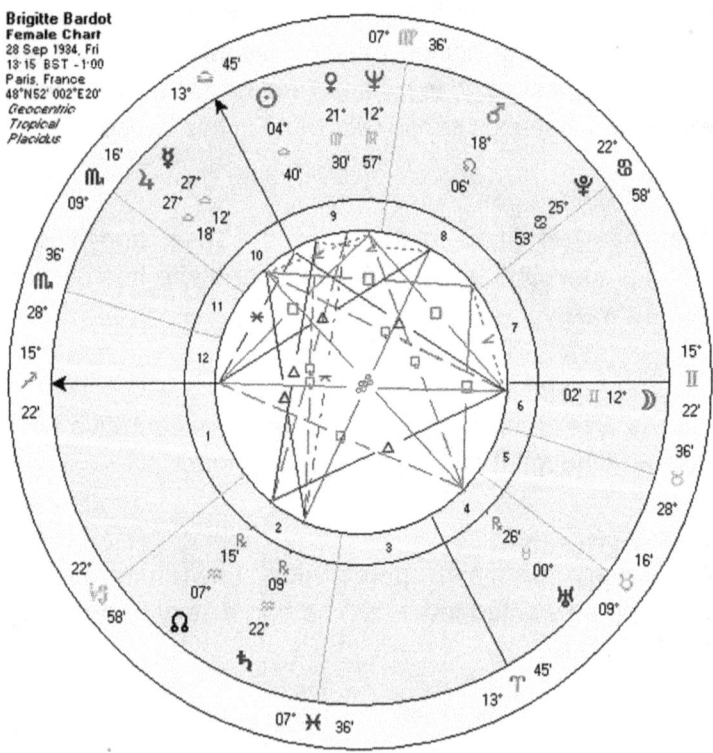

10: Pluto

Here are a few notes for you to consider. Brigitte's rising sign is Sagittarius, suggesting a spiritual nature, which is also sunny and broadminded, and she would travel and become known to people of many nationalities. She is as well-known as an activist on behalf of animals as by her many films. She started life as a dancer, but it was her looks that projected her into mega-stardom. Her Sun is in Libra, a sign that produces many beautiful and talented people, and her Moon is in Gemini in the sixth house, which is a hard-working sign and house, but also one that shows she has a good brain. Her rising planet is Saturn, emphasizing the effort she had to put into everything in her life. I leave the rest to you to ponder...

11: Chiron

CHIRON

Orbit: *Approximately 51 Earth years.*
Symbolic ideas: *Wounds, healing, Music and Training for Combat.*

The dwarf planet, Chiron, is a fairly recent discovery as far as astrology is concerned, so much so that it was unknown to astrologers in my early days of working in the field. This is what we know of it now.

Things Associated With Chiron

Teaching and Learning
I have noticed that Chiron shows up when people study something, take training courses, brush up on something, or obtain the knowledge and qualifications they need. Some may start to teach or train others.

Emotional Pain and Psychological Wounds
Chiron's natal position shows where you have been hurt during childhood and youth.

Relationships and Pain
A partner can be hurtful or cause physical or mental pain.

Illness, Accidents and Pain
This could be any kind of affliction, but it often involves the legs or feet.

11 Chiron

Healing
This is conventional medicine and complementary medicine or therapies - also, psychotherapy, counselling and help of all kinds, including spiritual healing.

Learning Music and all forms of Armed and Unarmed Combat
This links to the legend of Chiron the centaur who taught these subjects. It does seem to have a slight effect on people's lives, though.

A Fight of Some Kind
Chiron transits can set off battles of all kinds.

Metal
No metals or elements are attached to Chiron.

Health
Tradition links this planet to the Achilles tendon, but anything to do with the feet and legs can be a problem when Chiron makes a transit.

Age 12 to 13
The Chiron Quarter-Return
This is when Chiron is square to its natal position, and obviously, it links with having to take a more serious attitude to school and education, along with the start of puberty. It is unlikely to be a time of major change, though.

Age 25 to 26
The Chiron Half-Return
This is a fairly happy time for most people, but you may become dissatisfied with your job or some other aspect of your life, and decide to go in a new direction that requires

study or training. Another possibility is taking up a new job where there is a lot to learn.

Age 38 to 39
The Chiron Quarter-Return
This is a time when youth is slipping away, and a more mature attitude is needed. There may be a change of direction at work or changes and adjustments within the family structure. Chiron won't cause a major change at this time, but Uranus might well stir the pot bringing sudden changes in direction.

Age 50 to 52
The Chiron Return
This is an eventful time when two things seem to happen. The first is that you may have some kind of accident or suffer severe pain of some kind. In my case, the many years that I had spent in front of a computer damaged my upper spine, causing nerves to become inflamed and muscles to tear. The pain was horrendous, and it comes back from time to time when I overwork or become stressed. My friend Anne hurt her foot at this time and needed an operation to free a nerve that had become trapped between two bones.

The second event is a problem with a marriage or a relationship. This may or may not bring the marriage to an end, but it certainly puts a strain on the situation and the person who is hurt never quite trusts the partner again. It can be caused by unfaithfulness, financial disloyalty, unpleasant and abusive behaviour and many other things.

Age 63 to 64
The Chiron Quarter-Return
This is a surprisingly tricky age when you may find yourself with a real fight on your hands. You will have to learn

11 Chiron

something important at this time. There are other planetary events hovering around at this age, so these might join with Chiron to produce a profound time of change. I have known marriages to break down at this time, but you may simply decide to retire from work. Some people move house at this time, choosing the house they want to live in for the rest of their lives.

Age 76 to 77
The Chiron Half-Return
This is a time when old age creeps up in the form of health problems, stopping work, losing loved ones, changing direction or a myriad of other possibilities. Some people will choose to live in sheltered housing or a residential home. The way everything works out depends on a person's natal chart as well as the person's choice of lifestyle.

Age 89 to 90
The Chiron Quarter-Return
Illness and loss are possible now, but so is a feeling that all passion has been spent, and there isn't much more to worry about.

12: Planetary Cycles Table

Planetary Cycles Table and some Random Ideas

I have repeated the Cycles table here to save you from having to flip back to the start of the book to consult it. The table shows the dates when changes occur. Notice, for instance, the events around the early forties, early sixties and mid-eighties when there are several planetary events going on at the same time, making these times extremely memorable.

Key to the Codes:
    R   Return
    HR   Half-Return
    QR   Quarter-Return
    ER   Eighth-Return

Planetary Cycles Table

Ages	Planets	Brief Interpretations
6	Jupiter HR	Education and sports or activities become important now. End of babyhood.
7 – 8	Saturn QR	Can bring major problems, especially concerning the child's father.
11 – 12	Jupiter R	Changes of school, fairly happy time, success and achievement, making new friends.
12 – 13	Chiron QR	Education and sport are important, some unhappiness.
14 – 15	Saturn HR	Growing up, puberty, becoming responsible for self.
18 – 19	Jupiter HR	Problems in education or love life but soon overcome.
20 – 21	Uranus QR	Big change, education, love, pregnancy, job improvement.
20 – 21	Neptune ER	Falling in love, pregnancy, happy time.
24 – 25	Jupiter R	Should be happy, successful time for career and personal life. May travel a bit now.
25 – 26	Chiron HR	Realisation that something needs to change, could be training for a better job.
29	Saturn R	Major turning point for good after difficult time. Growing up, parenthood, responsibility, work changes.
30	Jupiter HR	Coming to terms with changes going on. Productive time.

Astrological Cycles In Focus

Ages	Planets	Brief Interpretations
36	Jupiter R	Major decisions, often related to childbirth.
38 – 39	Chiron QR	Irritating time when problems start to surface.
39 – 40	Uranus HR	Major change of direction.
41 – 42	Neptune QR	A stressful time at home or work. Health may be a problem.
42	Jupiter HR	Money may be a problem, or luck may be against the person.
40 – 45	Pluto QR	A time of transformation, which could go in any direction, but comes right after a period of difficulty.
44 – 45	Saturn HR	A heavy responsibility lands on the person. Must face up to reality.
48	Jupiter R	A time of happiness, expansion and something new which could be very successful.
50 – 52	Chiron R	A difficult time for health, accidents and trouble in love life and personal relationships. Change of life for women.
54	Jupiter HR	A somewhat tricky time when travel and foreigners could cause problems. Health may be a problem.
56 – 58	Saturn R	A time of realisation that things must change. Maybe retirement, something new, reward for effort but also sadness as things come to an end.
60	Jupiter R	A good time with more spirituality, travel perhaps, fun and joy.

Planetary Cycles Table

Ages	Planets	Brief Interpretations
62 – 63	Neptune ER	Spirituality develops, people show kindness, but muddles and even swindles can occur behind the person's back.
63	Uranus QR	A battle may need to be fought and a new attitude taken. Something must change.
63 – 64	Chiron QR	Health may be a problem now, and the subject needs to get a grip in many areas of life.
66	Jupiter HR	A time to face up to the need for change and a new direction.
72	Jupiter R	A productive time with new interests and a measure of success. Some travel or foreign friendships.
72	Saturn HR	Facing up to reality, maybe move of house or other practical matters.
76 – 77	Chiron HR	Health may be a problem now.
78	Jupiter HR	Financial setback, or trouble connected to spiritual matters or foreigners.
82 – 83	Neptune HR	An unexpected and possibly unusual health problem.
84	Jupiter R	Time of success and achievement.
84	Uranus R	Sudden changes; could be very good but unsettling.
87 – 88	Saturn R	Facing up to some form of reality.

Astrological Cycles In Focus

Ages	Planets	Brief Interpretations
88 – 90	Chiron QR	Health issues and some sadness or loss.
96	Jupiter HR	Loss of some measure of independence, restriction.
102 – 103	Neptune ER	Spiritual matters become important, may pass over now.
102	Jupiter R	Drawing to the end of a long and interesting life, very interested in spiritual matters.

The Hubers

There was once a lovely couple called Bruno and Louise Huber, and they lived in Switzerland. They had some ideas that were different from those of standard astrology, and you may find one or two of interest. Firstly, the Hubers disagreed with the general notion that Saturn rules the father and the Moon rules the mother; they reversed the system, saying that it was the mother who laid down the law and disciplined the children, while the father turned up every now and again and spoiled them or took them out to play games.

As it happens, ancient astrology considered the Sun the ruler of the father and the Moon to represent the mother, and that also has some value. In my case, I tend to use Saturn as the stricter parent or parent figure, whoever that may be, and the Moon to represent the nurturing influence, with the Sun also involved, whoever these people might be.

Another Huber idea was that life changes to some extent every six years, which of course is either the Jupiter

Planetary Cycles Table

return or its half-return, so it might be worth drawing up a six-yearly table and listing the things that happened to you to check out the theory.

Numerology

This is a completely different divination to astrology, but it also depends upon cycles; in this case, nine-year cycles, starting with the number one and ending with the number nine, then starting again at the number one. Make up a table of your life and see whether you had a new beginning every nine years. Also, check out the nature of each year as per the following list:

Year One:	Fresh start, new enthusiasm.
Year Two:	Partnership matters for love or work.
Year Three:	Creativity, fun.
Year Four:	Putting down roots, domestic life.
Year Five:	Restlessness, change, coping with difficulty.
Year Six:	Love but also duty and family life.
Year Seven:	Rest and spirituality.
Year Eight:	Work and success, social success.
Year Nine:	Winding things up, growing wiser.

Chinese Astrology

Chinese astrology brings us back to a somewhat vague orbit of Jupiter and Saturn, so this time, check out the situation every 12 years for Jupiter and every 30 years for Saturn in the Chinese system. Bear in mind that your year of birth is represented by an animal in the Chinese zodiac, which may be the Rat, the Ox, the Tiger, the Rabbit, the Dragon, the Snake, the Horse, the Goat, the Monkey, the Rooster, the Dog or the Pig.

Astrological Cycles In Focus

According to the Chinese tradition, every time you return to your own animal year sign (every 12 years), it will be a bad year for you. This is the direct opposite of the Western belief that the Jupiter return year should be a good time. Try the Chinese system for yourself and see where it gets you. You can find your animal year sign and much more about Chinese astrology online.

Conclusion

CONCLUSION

I wrote this book because I think it will be useful to those of you who are interested in what happens in your life. It will suit non-astrologers, along with those who are getting into astrology and those of you who are already deeply into the subject. The timing of planetary movement is a fascinating area to investigate, and it is an easy one to understand and to use. Indeed, you don't even need a birth chart to use this book, but of course, a natal chart will always add more substance because it will enable you to look at many kinds of transit in detail. I hope you have many happy hours looking into this subject and helping others to understand themselves and their life patterns.

May the stars be your guide.
Sasha Fenton

Index

Astrological Cycles In Focus

A
Ali, Mohammed 76
Amelia 85
Anderson, Pamela 38
aphelion 112
aphrodisiacs 44
Archer, Jeffrey 89
Assolant, Alfred 99
Astrolabe World Ephemeris 10

B
Bardot, Bridget 115
Bogarde, Dirk 116
Borg, Bjorn 76

C
Caduceus 35
Caine, Michael 115
Cameron, David 88
Casablanca 104
Castle, Barbara 46
Ceres 43
chakras, higher 103
Chan, Jackie 76
Charon 112
Chinese astrology 72
Chinese Astrology 131
Collins, Joan 115
conjunctions 11
Connors, Jimmy 56
Copper 45
Cromwell, Oliver 98

D
Dan 37
Depardieu, Gerald 99
Dietrich, Marlene 99
duck 37
Duke of Edinburgh 87

E
elephants, pewter 43
Exupery, Antoine de Saint 99

G
Gaulle, Charles de 98
Grant, Cary 88, 116
Grant, Russell 88

H
half-returns 11
Half-Returns 26
Helena's story 75
Hepburn, Audrey 99
Himmler, Heinrich 99
Hubers, The 130

J
Jane and Me 65
Jolene 53
Jonathan 66
Jones, Anthony Armstrong 98

K
Karma 79

Index

King, Billie Jean 76

L
Lisa's Story 86

M
Magna Carta 61
Melvin 95
Melvin's Story 95
meteorite 106
Moore, Tom 87
Morpheus 102
Mountbatten, Louis 104

N
Nicholson, Jack 115
Numerology 131

O
Oberon 102
Olivier, Lawrence 115
oppositions 11

P
Parton, Dolly 53, 109
perihelion 112
personal planet 26, 42, 50
Plutonium 114
Prince Charles 104
Princess Diana 104

Q
quarter-returns 11, 26
Queen Elizabeth 87
Queen Mother 109

quicksilver 34

R
Rachel's Story 85
retrograde motion 28
Retrograde, Jupiter 63
Retrograde, Mars 55
Retrograde, Venus 45
returns 11

S
Sarah 113
Sarah's Story 113
Saturday 29
Smith, Gordon Arthur 85
Solar Returns 26
solar system 18
Spears, Britney 109
Spitz, Mark 88
square aspects 26
squares 11
Stallone, Sylvester 29
Susan 96
Susan's Story 96
Swift, Taylor 109

T
Thatcher, Margaret 88
Theroux, Paul 99
third quarter-return 27
Titania 102
Tom, Captain 109
transpersonal planet 60, 78

~ 137 ~

Astrological Cycles In Focus

W
Walesa, Lech 88
Wicca 36

www.ingramcontent.com/pod-product-compliance
Lightning Source LLC
Chambersburg PA
CBHW070546090426
42735CB00013B/3086